PONDER

A

take up & READ

PUBLICATION

Managing Editor: Elizabeth Foss

Research & Development: Elizabeth Foss, Emily DeArdo

Copy Editors: Emily DeArdo, Rosie Hill

Cover Art and Illustration by: Katrina Harrington

Calligraphy by: Rakhi McCormick

Design by: Kristin Foss

ISBN-13: 978-1984162113

ISBN-10: 198416211X

take up & READ

C O M M U N I T Y

VISIT US

takeupandread.org

BE SOCIAL

Facebook @takeupandread

Instagram @takeupandread

Twitter @totakeupandread

SEND A NOTE

totakeupandread@gmail.com

CONNECT

#TakeUpAndRead

#PonderStudy

TO PONDER

This book began with a text message. My friend Kim, inspired by her daily time in a Take Up & Read study, asked me, "Do you have written down anywhere how to say the rosary each day? I want to do it later in the morning, but I am at the studio already. Anything written down I can follow?" Kim works long, twelve-hour days as the director of my daughters' dance school. She lives and breathes in the heart of constant music and motion. When she leaves the quiet of her home in the morning, she moves into a world that pulses with rhythm. Something in her time with God in the quiet was compelling her to seek Him in the noise of her workaday world and to find a rhythm there, too. Something in her Scripture study was bringing her to the rosary.

I knew there were books I could share and I did. I also shared my favorite rosary app. The rest of that conversation stayed with me, though. I was acutely aware that my language for sharing the devotion was limited. I knew the whats and the whys of the rosary. I could speak to the history of it. But how did it fit the life my friend leads? Where was the place for the rosary for a woman whose life is busy and noisy? Further, where was the rosary in the context of simple, beautiful Scripture studies that we publish?

I pondered that question a step at a time, literally thinking about the text conversation as I ran. The rhythm of my feet, the sound of my breath, the cadence and music of that run: it was simple, beautiful, and focused on what God was saying. Frequently, I find that I am best able to focus and to concentrate when I am moving in rhythm. Praying the rosary is a lot like a good run, or even a well-executed dance. The rosary is "Scripture on a string," each bead marking a place in in the Bible. But it is more than that. It is the rhythmic contemplation of mysteries of Christ's story. It is "the epitome of the whole Gospel" (CCC 971). The repeated prayers set the rhythm—the quiet cadence that brings us into

His presence. And the Scriptural stories of our Savior give us breath.

What you hold in your hands today is a book that seeks to create for you a place of pure beauty where you can find a simple rhythm with Our Lord. It's a book that seeks to honor the goodness of this prayer tradition and to bring each mystery to life for you in a personal, memorable way so that when you are finished, you will have engraved all of them on your heart and you will hold those memories now and in the future, when you sit (or stand or lie or run) to say the rosary.

Take each mystery a day a time. Get to know it well in your Bible. Look at it through the lens of each day's writer. Ponder it with your pen on the pages of this journal. And then pray it. Just that mystery if that is all you can manage—but give yourself the two or three minutes a day it takes to pray that one decade of the rosary. Our hope is that as the month progresses, each bead will become its own precious, personal symbol for you—forevermore reminding you of how you encountered Jesus in His Word when you studied that mystery.

When you reach the end of the book, you will have strung Scripture on a simple, but beautiful, string. You will have become intimate with these twenty mysteries, but there will always be so much more about them to know. Keep praying them. Keep listening to what He is saying in them. Our hope, and indeed our prayer, is that when this study ends you will have found or furthered a lifelong habit of pondering those mysteries in your heart, taking up the rhythm of blessed beads, even in the noise and the motion of your everyday life. Our hope is that this is just the beginning of a daily conversation with Jesus, counting beads and recalling the gift of His story.

Elizabeth Foss
Founder and Chief Content Director

THE ART

Dear Sisters,

When I set out to create the cover and interior artwork for *Ponder*, I wanted to create a huge array of roses, as each rosary is, in fact, a prayerful bouquet of roses to our Lady! The word rosary comes from the Latin *rosarium,* which means "garland of roses". The cover includes fifty-three roses to represent the fifty-three Hail Mary prayers sent up to heaven during a rosary. The leaves on the roses add up to 219 leaves as a nod to Luke 2:19, a passage that has been close to my heart this year, as well as the inspiration for the title of this study, Ponder. If you look closely at the center of each rose, you'll spot either a J, L, S, or G. These letters stand for Joyful, Luminous, Sorrowful, and Glorious—the four sets of mysteries we meditate upon as we pray a rosary.

For the interior artwork, I wanted to incorporate the somewhat lost tradition of Marian flowers that dates back to the Middle Ages. During the Age of Faith, flowers had religious names such as Mary's Gold, Mary's Shoes, or Pentecost Rose. Each set of mysteries in this book comes with a drawing combining flowers with religious names that can be associated with the mysteries. I pray that these drawings and the information they teach will prompt you to think of the rosary whenever you see one of the flowers in the wild! All of creation calls us to see God.

On the centerpiece of the rosary is a rose to represent Our Lady, the Mystical Rose, the rose in which the Divine Word became flesh. The "R" in the center of the rose stands for rosary, of course, and the ten thorns along the stem, the same number of Hail Mary prayers in each decade.

I hope these hidden meanings in each piece of art draw you deeper into prayer and remind you to find the hidden beauty in your life. Thank you for joining in on this study, a giant bouquet delivery to Mary, Our Mother. "He who finds Mary finds life, that is, Jesus Christ who is the way, the truth and the life." (St. Louis de Montfort)

Pax Christi,
Katrina, Artist of Rose Harrington

THE CALLIGRAPHY

When the team at Take Up & Read asked me to provide
the calligraphy for *Ponder*, I knew immediately I had to say
yes, and almost just as immediately knew which direction
the artwork would go. To honor the beauty and serenity of
the Blessed Mother, and to complement Katrina's beautiful
floral illustrations, the Spirit led me to draw with long,
flowing strokes. As the words came to life under my hand, it
was as though Mary's mantle was covering our pages as well
as my heart. The verses chosen by the team speak of hope,
of surrender, of salvation. My prayer is that these pages of
calligraphy give you space to ponder the immense gift that we
have in Christ, the powerful witness we have in the Blessed
Mother, and the magnificent beauty with which you were
created in Him.

Rakhi McCormick, Calligrapher of Rakstar Designs

But Mary treasured all these words & pondered them in her heart.

LUKE 2:19

HOW TO PRAY THE ROSARY

The rosary is made up of twenty decades of ten Hail Marys, each decade focusing on a mystery—an incident in the life of Mary or Jesus.

The mysteries are broken into four categories:

the **Joyful Mysteries**, which focus on the early life of Jesus
the **Luminous Mysteries**, where we meditate on Jesus' public life
the **Sorrowful Mysteries**, to contemplate Jesus' Passion and death
and the **Glorious Mysteries**, which celebrate His resurrection and the early life of the Church.

The Hail Marys that make up each decade provide the rhythm and the background music for our meditation on the mysteries.

Physical rosaries can be ornate, or as simple as a ring around your finger to help you pray during your commute. Usually, a set of rosary beads consists of fifty-five beads, divided into five sets of mysteries, with a small strand of beads for the introductory prayers that ends in a crucifix. The beads for the Our Fathers are usually larger, giving you a tactile reminder that you've reached the end of a decade.

To pray the rosary, you begin with introductory prayers: Make the sign of the cross while holding the crucifix at the end of the rosary. Then, say the Apostles' Creed. On the first large bead, pray the Our Father. On each of the three smaller beads that follow, pray a Hail Mary. Then, on the last large bead in the sequence, pray a Glory Be.

Rosaries have a centerpiece that connects the small strand of beads to the circular rosary. On this piece (it can be a bead, a medal, or just a simple knot), you'll begin your meditations. Choose a set of mysteries to pray that day. There are traditional assignments for the days of the week: the Joyful Mysteries are prayed on Monday and Saturday, the Luminous on Thursday, the Sorrowful on Tuesday and Friday, and the Glorious on Wednesday and Sunday. You can choose to follow this, or pray whatever mysteries are speaking to your heart that day.

On the centerpiece, announce (even internally, to yourself) the first mystery of the set you've chosen. Pray the Our Father. Then move to the ten Hail Mary beads. As you pray, contemplate the mystery you've chosen. You can do this by imagining the scene. You might read a book of rosary meditations or use another contemplative aid to help you focus and ponder. Sometimes you'll be too tired, sad, or sick to focus deeply on meditation. Those are the days when the rhythm of the familiar prayers bring you into the presence of Jesus and Mary. You can also offer each decade for a particular intention, and focus your prayer and meditation there.

Upon finishing the ten Hail Marys, you'll come to another large bead. Here, say the Glory Be. In some traditions, the O My Jesus is said here also.

After you complete one mystery of the rosary, if that's all you plan to say, end with the Hail, Holy Queen. If you're going to continue, announce the second mystery, pray another Our Father, and continue the cycle.

At the conclusion of the set of mysteries, you will be back at the starting centerpiece. If you're saying more than one set of mysteries, simply begin with the next mystery here. If you're completing your daily time with the rosary, here say the Hail, Holy Queen and make the sign of the cross.

PRAYERS OF THE ROSARY

The Apostles' Creed

I believe in God,
the Father almighty,
Creator of heaven and earth,
and in Jesus Christ, His only Son, our Lord,
who was conceived by the Holy Spirit,
born of the Virgin Mary,
suffered under Pontius Pilate,
was crucified, died and was buried;
he descended into hell;
on the third day he rose again from the dead;
he ascended into heaven,
and is seated at the right hand of God the Father almighty;
from there he will come to judge the living and the dead.

I believe in the Holy Spirit,
the holy catholic Church,
the communion of saints,
the forgiveness of sins,
the resurrection of the body,
and life everlasting.
Amen.

The Our Father

Our Father, who art in heaven,
hallowed be thy name;
thy kingdom come;
thy will be done on earth as it is in heaven.
Give us this day our daily bread;
and forgive us our trespasses
as we forgive those who trespass
against us;
and lead us not into temptation,
but deliver us from evil. (Matthew 6:9-13)
Amen.

The Hail Mary

Hail Mary, full of grace, the Lord is with you; (Luke 1:28)
blessed are you among women, (Luke 1:41-42a, Luke 1:48)
and blessed is the fruit of your womb, Jesus. (Luke 1:42b)
Holy Mary, Mother of God, (Luke 1:43)
pray for us sinners
now and at the hour of our death. (Luke 2:35, John 2:5,
Rev. 2:10)
Amen.

The Glory Be (The Doxology)

Glory be to the Father, and to the Son, and to the Holy Spirit;
as it was in the beginning, is now, and ever shall be,
world without end. (Romans 11:33-36)
Amen.

The O My Jesus (Fatima Prayer)

O my Jesus, forgive us our sins, save us from the fires of hell,
and lead all souls to Heaven, especially those in most need
of Your Mercy.

The Hail Holy Queen (The Salve Regina)

Hail, holy Queen, mother of mercy,
our life, our sweetness, and our hope.
To you do we cry, poor banished children of Eve;
to you do we send up our sighs,
mourning and weeping in this valley of tears.
Turn, then, most gracious advocate,
your eyes of mercy toward us;
and after this, our exile,
show unto us the blessed fruit of your womb, Jesus.
O clement, O loving, O sweet Virgin Mary.
Pray for us, O Holy Mother of God,
that we may be made worthy of the promises of Christ.

Concluding Prayer of the Rosary

Let us pray. O God, whose only begotten Son, by His life, death, and resurrection, has purchased for us the rewards of eternal life, grant, we beseech Thee, that meditating upon these mysteries of the Most Holy Rosary of the Blessed Virgin Mary, we may imitate what they contain and obtain what they promise, through the same Christ Our Lord.

Amen.

ROSARY MAP

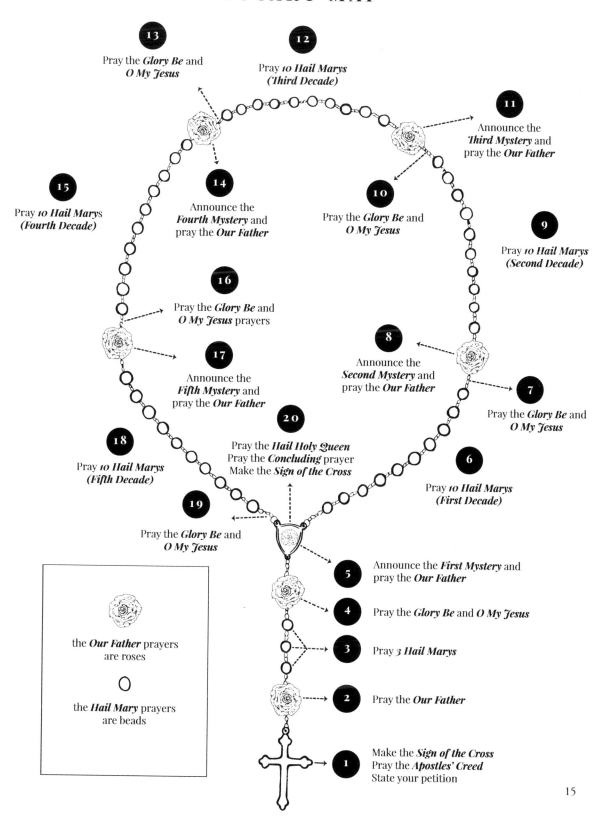

13 Pray the *Glory Be* and *O My Jesus*

12 Pray *10 Hail Marys* (*Third Decade*)

11 Announce the *Third Mystery* and pray the *Our Father*

15 Pray *10 Hail Marys* (*Fourth Decade*)

14 Announce the *Fourth Mystery* and pray the *Our Father*

10 Pray the *Glory Be* and *O My Jesus*

9 Pray *10 Hail Marys* (*Second Decade*)

16 Pray the *Glory Be* and *O My Jesus* prayers

17 Announce the *Fifth Mystery* and pray the *Our Father*

8 Announce the *Second Mystery* and pray the *Our Father*

7 Pray the *Glory Be* and *O My Jesus*

20 Pray the *Hail Holy Queen* Pray the *Concluding* prayer Make the *Sign of the Cross*

18 Pray *10 Hail Marys* (*Fifth Decade*)

6 Pray *10 Hail Marys* (*First Decade*)

19 Pray the *Glory Be* and *O My Jesus*

5 Announce the *First Mystery* and pray the *Our Father*

4 Pray the *Glory Be* and *O My Jesus*

3 Pray *3 Hail Marys*

2 Pray the *Our Father*

1 Make the *Sign of the Cross* Pray the *Apostles' Creed* State your petition

the *Our Father* prayers are roses

O

the *Hail Mary* prayers are beads

15

INTENTIONAL DESIGN

Each of our studies is created with unique, intentional design. We want to connect you with the Word and keep you connected throughout the day. In this Scripture study, we provided scholarly research to guide you through the ancient practice of *lectio divina* ("holy reading"). For detailed guidance on *lectio divina*, please see page 156. Fresh layouts, font design, and original artwork ensure that you have the tools to keep Him close to your heart, every day.

DAILY SCRIPTURE READING

This Scripture study includes daily Scripture readings. Notations for further reading are provided so you can open your Bible and further explore the Word.

LECTIO DIVINA

Reflect upon the Word and make a deep connection with your daily life.

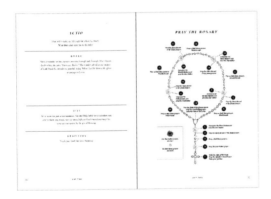

ACTIO

Follow the action plan with Grace, Gift and space for Gratitude.

PRAY THE ROSARY

Each day, we encourage you to pray the rosary by offering a blank, illustrated rosary to meditate with.

WEEKLY SCRIPTURE VERSE

In this book, we will work on memorizing one key verse to reflect each week's mysteries.

SELAH

Here is a chance to pause for prayer, praise, and rest.

At Take Up & Read, we want you to discover what prompts and pages are most useful to you. There is no perfect way to perform lectio—the important thing is that you take the time to have a conversation with God, using His Word as your guide.

LECTIO PAGE IN ACTION

2 Timothy 3:16-17
Written by St. Paul from prison to St. Timothy, who was in Ephesus.
"All scripture" means all of the Old Testament but also maybe some
of the Gospel accounts that became part of the New Testament.

MEDITATIO	What personal message does the text have for me?	The social media feeds I choose can compete with the message of the gospel. Scripture can be trusted. It should be my go-to when preparing for every<u>thing</u>, my inspiration more than the internet.
ORATIO	What do I say to the Lord in response to His word?	Thank you for giving for giving me your Word. Remind me through out my day, when I lose my way and look to other sources of direction, that You have everything I need to do Your good work.
CONTEMPLATIO	What conversion of mind, heart, and life is He asking of me today?	I think God is reminding me to get the ratio right: consult Scripture more than other things that compete for my time and attention.

How did I progress in living the Word today?

THE

JOYFUL MYSTERIES

WEEKLY SCRIPTURE MEMORY

THE JOYFUL MYSTERIES

When we memorize Scripture, we imitate Jesus, who hid God's Word in His heart and who proclaimed it even in His most sorrowful agony. As He hung in the final moments of His life, Scripture was the last thing on his breath, and Jesus, "crying with a loud voice, said, 'Father, into your hands I commend my spirit.' Having said this, He breathed his last." (Luke 23:46) We can almost certainly know that Jesus learned those words (from Psalm 31) from His mother as a prayer when He was a little boy. She poured into Him a treasury of Scripture and He knew just where to find it all His life.

To hold the Word so close and so dear that it is what sustains us in the very last moments of our life! To hide the Lord in our hearts in such a real and present way that He spills out into our speech when we are neediest and when we are most joyful! These are the true goals of the Take Up & Read studies.

Each week, we offer a memory verse for you to hide in your hearts, and perhaps in the hearts of children, too. This week, we focus on the canticle of Simeon, which he prayed upon seeing the baby Jesus when Mary and Joseph presented Him in the temple forty days after His birth. This hymn of praise is prayed around the world every night during Compline, or Night Prayer.

Perhaps you can repeat it to yourself as you fall asleep, relinquishing your will to the Lord and trusting that He will keep His promises to you.

Luke 2:28-32

Simeon took him in his arms and praised God, saying,
  "Master, now you are dismissing your servant in peace,
    according to your word;
for my eyes have seen your salvation,
which you have prepared in the presence of all peoples,
a light for revelation to the Gentiles
    and for glory to your people Israel."

My eyes have seen Your salvation

LUKE 2:30

LUKE 1:26-38

In the sixth month the angel Gabriel was sent by God to a town in Galilee called Nazareth, to a virgin engaged to a man whose name was Joseph, of the house of David. The virgin's name was Mary. And he came to her and said, "Greetings, favored one! The Lord is with you." But she was much perplexed by his words and pondered what sort of greeting this might be. The angel said to her, "Do not be afraid, Mary, for you have found favor with God. And now, you will conceive in your womb and bear a son, and you will name him Jesus. He will be great, and will be called the Son of the Most High, and the Lord God will give to him the throne of his ancestor David. He will reign over the house of Jacob forever, and of his kingdom there will be no end." Mary said to the angel, "How can this be, since I am a virgin?" The angel said to her, "The Holy Spirit will come upon you, and the power of the Most High will overshadow you; therefore the child to be born will be holy; he will be called Son of God. And now, your relative Elizabeth in her old age has also conceived a son; and this is the sixth month for her who was said to be barren. For nothing will be impossible with God." Then Mary said, "Here am I, the servant of the Lord; let it be with me according to your word." Then the angel departed from her.

TO PONDER: Genesis 18: 9-14

LECTIO DIVINA

THE ANNUNCIATION | LUKE 1:26-28

LECTIO

The account of the Annunciation is only found in Luke's Gospel. Written for Gentile Christians sometime in the 80s A.D., Luke gives us a powerful and unique portrait of Mary not found in the other gospels. Here, the angel Gabriel has told Mary that God has chosen her to be the mother of His Son. By her selfless "yes," Mary becomes a model for faithful, generous obedience to God's will.

MEDITATIO

What personal message does the text have for me?

ORATIO

What do I say to the Lord in response to His word?

CONTEMPLATIO

What conversion of mind, heart, and life is He asking of me today?

How did I progress in living the Word today?

THE FIRST JOYFUL MYSTERY:
THE ANNUNCIATION

After finishing chemotherapy, my doctors warned me that I
might not be able to have more children. I was crushed. But
four years later, by the grace of God, I'd finally found peace
in the size of our little family—just the three of us. Then, I
was surprised by joy when I learned that I was pregnant once
again.

I found out in the morning, when my husband was at
work. It was hard to wait to tell him; and yet, there was also
something beautiful about the hours when only I had the
news. For I knew that once I said it out loud to someone
else, the necessary questions about practical matters and their
accompanying anxieties would soon follow.

As is so often the case, it seemed that there were countless
things to worry about. For one, my husband had just taken a
government job with a pay cut, long hours, and no time off.
For another, the traumatic experience I'd had with pregnancy
and birth the first time around threatened to stir up worries
and fears I'd worked hard to overcome.

But on the day I got our good news, none of that mattered.
Instead, my heart was filled with joy and an abiding sense
of peace—an understanding that all the difficult things I'd
endured and all the difficult things that were to come were no
match for God, for whom all things are possible.

Knowing how I felt that day, I can only begin to imagine the
joy Mary felt at the annunciation. How incredible it must
have been to hear that she, a young girl of humble stature,
was favored by God! How incredible to be invited to help
bring our Savior into the world.

When the angel Gabriel announces the good news to Mary,
he doesn't tell her how everything will play out. And yet, she

still chooses to trust God and say "yes" to His plan, changing her life and the world in an instant. Then, just like that, "the angel departed from her."

Life seems to move on rather quickly, and, after Jesus' birth, we hear only a few stories about Mary. We don't know all that happened as she raised her Son. But even before she watched Him suffer and die on the cross, it's likely that there were more than a few challenging moments along the way.

After the initial joy at the news of my pregnancy, my family also encountered challenges. Some were those I'd expected, and others came as surprises, like the freezing water that poured out of a burst pipe and filled our house as we slept one night. When we realized what was happening, my husband struggled to stop the water, and I struggled to carry my sleeping son to the one remaining dry room. My legs throbbed from the extra weight of both children that I carried, and all I could do was cry.

Life will inevitably bring us challenges—sometimes for just a moment, and sometimes for much longer. But like Mary, we are called to say yes to God's will each and every day, even when we are standing ankle-deep in freezing water and our bodies ache from the weight of all we carry. And it is precisely in those moments, when we feel ourselves moving away from God and into darkness, that we must remember the moments of joy God has given us, too.

Like Mary, let us treasure everything that God has generously provided—His holy Word, our callings, and the moments when we've been filled with His grace. And let us ponder these things in our hearts often, so that even when we face challenges, we never forget how deeply God loves us and how He delights in surprising us with joy.

Allison McGinley

ACTIO

How will I make my life a gift for others in charity?
What does God want me to do today?

GRACE

There is wonder in this mystery, wonder through and through. Mary doesn't doubt when she says, "How can this be?" She wonders aloud at the majesty of God. Find the wonder in your life today. Where has He shown His glory in unexpected ways?

GIFT

Sit in quiet for just a few moments. Ask the Holy Spirit to overshadow you and to show you where you can shine light on God's wondrous ways for someone else today. Be the gift of blessing.

GRATITUDE

Thank you, Lord, for these blessings:

PRAY THE ROSARY

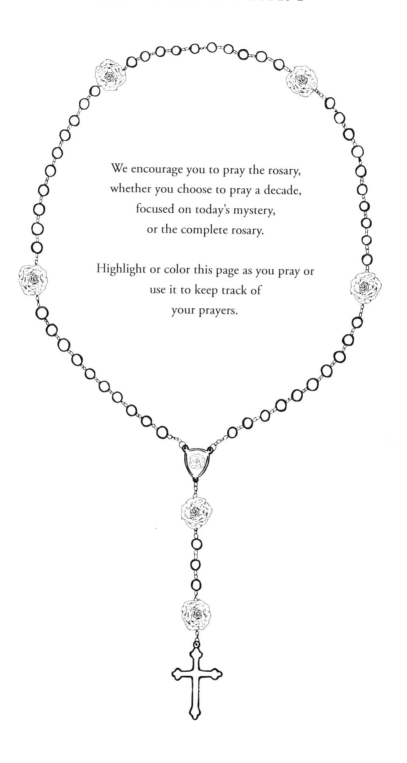

We encourage you to pray the rosary,
whether you choose to pray a decade,
focused on today's mystery,
or the complete rosary.

Highlight or color this page as you pray or
use it to keep track of
your prayers.

TAKE UP AND READ

DAY THREE

LUKE 1:39-56

In those days Mary set out and went with haste to a Judean town in the hill country, where she entered the house of Zechariah and greeted Elizabeth. When Elizabeth heard Mary's greeting, the child leaped in her womb. And Elizabeth was filled with the Holy Spirit and exclaimed with a loud cry, "Blessed are you among women, and blessed is the fruit of your womb. And why has this happened to me, that the mother of my Lord comes to me? For as soon as I heard the sound of your greeting, the child in my womb leaped for joy. And blessed is she who believed that there would be a fulfillment of what was spoken to her by the Lord."

And Mary said,
"My soul magnifies the Lord,
 and my spirit rejoices in God my Savior,
for he has looked with favor on the lowliness of his servant.
  Surely, from now on all generations will call me blessed;
for the Mighty One has done great things for me,
  and holy is his name.
His mercy is for those who fear him
  from generation to generation.
He has shown strength with his arm;
  he has scattered the proud in the thoughts of their hearts.
He has brought down the powerful from their thrones,
  and lifted up the lowly;
he has filled the hungry with good things,
  and sent the rich away empty.
He has helped his servant Israel,
  in remembrance of his mercy,
according to the promise he made to our ancestors,
  to Abraham and to his descendants forever."
And Mary remained with her about three months and then returned to her home.

TO PONDER: Luke 1:8-25, 1 Samuel 2:1-10, 2 Samuel 6

    DAY THREE

LECTIO DIVINA

THE VISITATION | LUKE 1:39-56

LECTIO

Luke's Gospel is considered the most literary Gospel, and his account of the visitation gives weight to that assertion. Upon visiting her cousin Elizabeth, who is pregnant with John the Baptist, Mary prays her beautiful Magnificat, where she praises God's faithfulness and mercy toward His people.

MEDITATIO

What personal message does the text have for me?

ORATIO

What do I say to the Lord in response to His word?

CONTEMPLATIO

What conversion of mind, heart, and life is He asking of me today?

How did I progress in living the Word today?

THE SECOND JOYFUL MYSTERY: THE VISITATION

One of the mysteries of my soul is that whenever I am at a loss for words I default to Marian prayers. I didn't grow up reciting the rosary. When I was given a rosary for my First Communion, I broke it trying to fit it over my head. I thought it was a necklace. And then I lost it. I didn't cultivate a rosary habit until much, much later. So, why is it that when I have no words, the words of Elizabeth come spilling out? Why do I seem to default to praying the Scriptures of the first two joyful mysteries of the rosary?

To be clear, I'm not praying to Mary. I'm asking Mary to pray for me. Just as I might text a friend and beg for prayers in the moment, I know that in the great cloud of witnesses that surrounds me, Mary stands radiant. She is my best prayer warrior and advocate: always available, always tender, always trustworthy. I am Elizabeth (in more ways than one), and she never comes to me alone. She comes bearing Jesus.

In a way, we repeat the first two mysteries with every decade. When we say the words of Gabriel, and Elizabeth, and Mary herself, we are brought to the holy moments of greeting. In the happy exchange between Mary and Elizabeth, we recognize Mary as a channel of grace. Just as Jesus is carried by Mary to sanctify Saint John the Baptist, she carries Him to me.

When the angel Gabriel visited Zechariah, he told the old man that his baby boy would be filled with the Holy Spirit from the womb. Young Mary, who is filled to brimming over with the Holy Spirit, calls out a warm hello and Elizabeth says, "as soon as I heard the sound of your greeting, the child in my womb leaped for joy." Mary brings the joy of the Lord to Elizabeth, to baby John, and to us. Indeed, the sweet mother of Jesus is so joyful that she breaks into a glorious song of praise.

In the Magnificat, we see a tapestry of Mary's soul woven with threads of ancient Scripture. A young woman of mature faith, she is so imbued with holy Scripture that her words move in and out of Hannah's song (1 Samuel 1:2-10), leaving the listener to wonder where Mary ends and the Scripture begins. Her thoughts are given voice with the words of God and she is, quite literally, one with the Word. This is the faith that allowed her to hope.

In hope, she gave her fiat. She believed God's promises taught to her from the Scriptures, and so she assented in humility when the angel asked her receive the Holy Spirit. Still, she sees herself only as the handmaiden of God, there to play her part in God's plan. Full of this hope, Mary answers God's call to visit Elizabeth and, with prayer and service, brings God Himself to her cousin.

Her mission to Elizabeth is one of charity and her song is one of love. Her will perfectly joined with her Creator's, she carries His love with humility and gentleness. She will remain with our Lord for His lifetime, always a handmaiden, always pointing towards God. We can trust her to take us to Him.

Even as they've gotten older, I notice that when my children are in trouble—when they know they're in over their heads and they understand that they need adult wisdom (and possibly chastisement)—they invariably come to me first. But it's their dad they know they will eventually meet in the matter. I am but a conduit to the greater conversation. Maybe this phenomenon explains my own reflex to call upon Mary first. I come to her for good and gentle counsel, but my soul also knows that it is through my most holy Mother that I will best meet my Father.

Elizabeth Foss

ACTIO

How will I make my life a gift for others in charity?
What does God want me to do today?

GRACE

Pull your favorite phrases from the Magnificat. Write them here. Repeat
them to yourself until they become a part of you.

GIFT

Visit someone today. It doesn't have to be fancy or take a long time; just
show up at someone's doorstep with a spring bouquet or a latte—and bring
Jesus. Smile. Offer warmth and light.

GRATITUDE

Thank you, Lord, for these blessings:

PRAY THE ROSARY

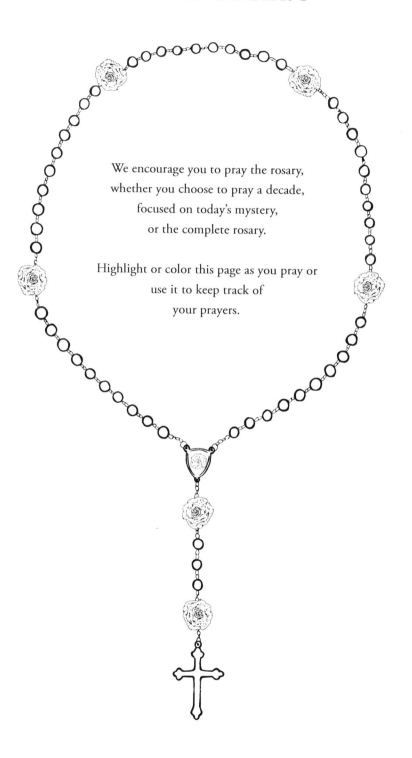

We encourage you to pray the rosary,
whether you choose to pray a decade,
focused on today's mystery,
or the complete rosary.

Highlight or color this page as you pray or
use it to keep track of
your prayers.

DAY FOUR

LUKE 2:1-20

In those days a decree went out from Emperor Augustus that all the world should be registered. This was the first registration and was taken while Quirinius was governor of Syria. All went to their own towns to be registered. Joseph also went from the town of Nazareth in Galilee to Judea, to the city of David called Bethlehem, because he was descended from the house and family of David. He went to be registered with Mary, to whom he was engaged and who was expecting a child. While they were there, the time came for her to deliver her child. And she gave birth to her firstborn son and wrapped him in bands of cloth, and laid him in a manger, because there was no place for them in the inn.

In that region there were shepherds living in the fields, keeping watch over their flock by night. Then an angel of the Lord stood before them, and the glory of the Lord shone around them, and they were terrified. But the angel said to them, "Do not be afraid; for see—I am bringing you good news of great joy for all the people: to you is born this day in the city of David a Savior, who is the Messiah, the Lord. This will be a sign for you: you will find a child wrapped in bands of cloth and lying in a manger." And suddenly there was with the angel a multitude of the heavenly host, praising God and saying,

"Glory to God in the highest heaven,
    and on earth peace among those whom he favors!"

When the angels had left them and gone into heaven, the shepherds said to one another, "Let us go now to Bethlehem and see this thing that has taken place, which the Lord has made known to us." So they went with haste and found Mary and Joseph, and the child lying in the manger. When they saw this, they made known what had been told them about this child; and all who heard it were amazed at what the shepherds told them. But Mary treasured all these words and pondered them in her heart. The shepherds returned, glorifying and praising God for all they had heard and seen, as it had been told them.

TO PONDER: Isaiah 7:14

LECTIO DIVINA

THE NATIVITY | LUKE 2:1-20

The central theme of Luke's gospel is the universality of the Good News, and the unbounded offer of salvation to both Jews and Gentiles. With Jesus' birth, salvation is now possible; He will save humanity from sin and death. Bethlehem means "House of Bread"—a fitting birthplace for the one who will become the bread of life.

MEDITATIO

What personal message does the text have for me?

ORATIO

What do I say to the Lord in response to His word?

CONTEMPLATIO

What conversion of mind, heart, and life is He asking of me today?

How did I progress in living the Word today?

THE THIRD JOYFUL MYSTERY:
THE NATIVITY

Regardless of the circumstances, childbirth is an inherently potent means of detachment from physical comforts.

I have given birth without medication, had a planned cesarean section, and also had three epidural births. My first epidural birth was so effective that I felt nothing at all during the birthing process itself. In terms of alleviation of physical pain, I think I was the most comfortable I could have been in that situation. Still, I recall the fears, the difficulty of leaving my other little ones at home, the anxiety that compelled me to constantly stare at the heart rate of my yet-to-be-born baby girl on the monitor, the concern regarding her health after the birth. I remember alternating between feeling cold and feeling hot, and the vulnerability of putting myself entirely in the doctor's hands. Even in this most "ideal" birthing situation, I remained acutely aware of just how much was out of my control.

My own experiences of childbirth are certainly unlike that of our Lady and Saint Joseph, as is my level of detachment. I have never given birth in the middle of the night, in the piercing cold, outdoors, housed only by a stable (or cave), and surrounded by animals. I have never been turned away from the hospital when looking for an open birthing room. Mary and Joseph's total relinquishment of their comfort, of any feeling of control, of the way that they may have previously envisioned the birth of this promised Savior—in short, their total acceptance of the many wild cards of their situation—is a beautiful human example of detachment from the goods of this world for the sake of welcoming our Lord.

It is not just the physical detachment of Mary and Joseph that we can meditate upon, but also their spiritual surrender. They have worked to bring the Savior to birth precisely so that they can give Him to humanity, and this surrender continues, from His birth to the flight into Egypt, to the finding in the temple, all the way up to the cross. Mary and Joseph are called by God to a unique, constant cooperation with His will, so that His plan of salvation can unfold. Because of this call and their generous response, they are drawn into the mystery of Jesus Christ, God the Word incarnate, and as they were the instruments chosen by God to bring the Savior into the world, so too they continue even now to lead us to our Lord.

The poverty and complete humility that Mary and Joseph lived in the Nativity is like a magnet drawing us to the manger—they have decreased so that the glory of the newborn King may increase. In the mystery of the Nativity, Mary and Joseph are so emptied of themselves and full of love for our Lord that, as each one of us moves closer to the manger, they help to lead us to come and adore Him.

A favorite reflection of mine on this mystery is given by Saint Josemaría Escrivá in his work *The Holy Rosary,* where he says that our Lady and Saint Joseph stand by the manger in order to invite us to spend as much time with our Lord as we like. Saint Joseph hands the infant Jesus to us so that we can, in all tenderness and love, imitate Mary and himself in holding the divine infant close to our breasts, kissing Him, singing to Him, rocking Him, and worshipping Him, "call[ing] Him King, Love, my God, my Only-one, my All!"

If our hearts and arms are full of our human attachments—our physical comfort, our self-love, our unforgiveness, our vanity, our pride, our love of this world—then we have no room to hold our Lord with tender love and let Him fill us. Mary and Joseph show us the way to the Way.

Ana Hahn

ACTIO

How will I make my life a gift for others in charity?
What does God want me to do today?

GRACE

Imagine your response to the burdens of birth in a cave. How would you
meet the travel, the stench, the animals, the cold? How would you greet the
strangers: innkeepers, shepherds? As you ponder your place in the scene,
what do you hear God telling you about yourself?

GIFT

Visit a church today and sit in the presence of the Bread of Life. This is our
Bethlehem—our house of bread, our place of refuge and nourishment.

GRATITUDE

Thank you, Lord, for these blessings:

PRAY THE ROSARY

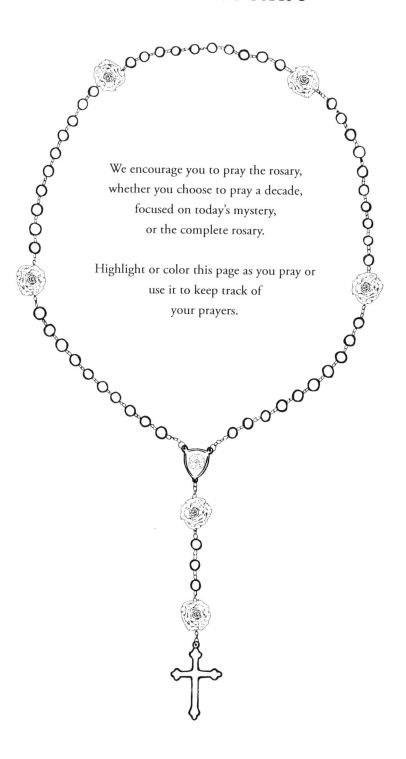

We encourage you to pray the rosary,
whether you choose to pray a decade,
focused on today's mystery,
or the complete rosary.

Highlight or color this page as you pray or
use it to keep track of
your prayers.

LUKE 2:22-38

When the time came for their purification according to the law of Moses, they brought him up to Jerusalem to present him to the Lord (as it is written in the law of the Lord, "Every firstborn male shall be designated as holy to the Lord"), and they offered a sacrifice according to what is stated in the law of the Lord, "a pair of turtledoves or two young pigeons."

Now there was a man in Jerusalem whose name was Simeon; this man was righteous and devout, looking forward to the consolation of Israel, and the Holy Spirit rested on him. It had been revealed to him by the Holy Spirit that he would not see death before he had seen the Lord's Messiah. Guided by the Spirit, Simeon came into the temple; and when the parents brought in the child Jesus, to do for him what was customary under the law, Simeon took him in his arms and praised God, saying,

"Master, now you are dismissing your servant in peace,
    according to your word;
for my eyes have seen your salvation,
    which you have prepared in the presence of all peoples,
a light for revelation to the Gentiles
    and for glory to your people Israel."

And the child's father and mother were amazed at what was being said about him. Then Simeon blessed them and said to his mother Mary, "This child is destined for the falling and the rising of many in Israel, and to be a sign that will be opposed so that the inner thoughts of many will be revealed—and a sword will pierce your own soul too."

There was also a prophet, Anna the daughter of Phanuel, of the tribe of Asher. She was of a great age, having lived with her husband seven years after her marriage, then as a widow to the age of eighty-four. She never left the temple but worshiped there with fasting and prayer night and day. At that moment she came, and began to praise God and to speak about the child to all who were looking for the redemption of Jerusalem.

TO PONDER: 2 Corinthians 2:7-15

LECTIO DIVINA

THE PRESENTATION IN THE TEMPLE | LUKE 2:22-38

The birth of a male child disqualified an Israelite woman from touching any holy object or approaching the Temple for forty days, after which time she must offer sacrifice in Jerusalem. The Holy Family offers the sacrifice of the poor: two turtle doves or pigeons. While Mary has no sin to atone for, she fulfils the requirements of her faith. Also, Jesus is consecrated to the Lord, either by being consecrated as a priest, or by being "bought" from the Levites for five shekels.

LECTIO

MEDITATIO

What personal message does the text have for me?

ORATIO

What do I say to the Lord in response to His word?

CONTEMPLATIO

What conversion of mind, heart, and life is He asking of me today?

How did I progress in living the Word today?

THE FOURTH JOYFUL MYSTERY:
THE PRESENTATION IN THE TEMPLE

I've always been captivated by the world C.S. Lewis created in his Narnia series. As a child, I wanted nothing more than to hear the voice of Aslan, to have tea with Mr. Tumnus, and to catch sight of a dryad on a spring morning. But it's a talking mouse who's taught me the most about how to live as a Christian.

Reepicheep and his companions have spent the entire *Voyage of the Dawn Treader* journeying east. He's looking for Aslan's country, for heaven. Towards the end of the book, the characters discuss plans to head for home. But Reepicheep isn't interested in turning back:

"My own plans are made. While I can, I sail east in the Dawn Treader. When she fails me, I paddle east in my coracle. When she sinks, I shall swim east with my four paws. And when I can swim no longer, if I have not reached Aslan's country, or shot over the edge of the world into some vast cataract, I shall sink with my nose to the sunrise."

Every time I read these words, I feel a fire in my bones. I want to long for heaven the way Reepicheep does. I want to fix my eyes on Jesus and run, swim, drift, drown even, always seeking Him.

This is why I love the presentation. For all I can meditate on Jesus being offered as a sacrifice, on Mary's surrender, on their faithfulness, it's Simeon who's captured my heart here.

We don't know much about Simeon. Does he have a job? A family? Does he, like Anna, spend every moment in the Temple worshipping? Or does he keep the word of God alive in his heart while going about his daily business?

It doesn't matter. Simeon isn't given to us as a prototype, with details we have to copy exactly. He's an image of what a heart fixed on the Father looks like. Simeon is, above all, a man who is waiting, longing for Emmanuel.

I imagine him, old and weak, gasping as he catches sight of the newborn Savior. I can see him struggling to his feet, shaking as he leans on his cane and hurries towards the Christ child. Then suddenly, his cane drops to the floor as he reaches out to grasp the baby. Tears stream down his face as he laughs for joy, holding tightly to the pudgy God-man.

As Joseph and Mary look on, he kisses God's face, breathes in His baby smell, and worships. Then, softly, he prays aloud, "Now, Master, you may let your servant go in peace." Oh, Father, he prays. That's all I need. You can bring me home now. There's nothing more this world could offer. I can die happy, he says. All because he met Jesus.

This is what I want. I want to receive him in the Eucharist with this joy. I want to find in this world only such gladness as makes me long for the next. Like Reepicheep, I know I'm a pilgrim. But sometimes I forget that this world is not my home.

That's the whole point of pondering, isn't it? When we live with our eyes only on this world, we begin to find ourselves in passing things. We see our work, our families, our communities as ends in themselves rather than creatures designed to show us the love of the Creator. But when we take time each day to recalibrate, to set our sights once more on the Love of which every human relationship is but a shadow, the good things of this world begin more and more to point us to the next.

You don't have to weep for joy every time you receive the Eucharist to be living like Simeon. You don't have to long for death. But if your heart isn't at least a little bit hungry for heaven, ask the Lord to give you the heart of Simeon or Reepicheep, pilgrims ready to go home.

Meg Hunter-Kilmer

ACTIO

How will I make my life a gift for others in charity?
What does God want me to do today?

GRACE

Ponder through the lens of Love today. Look at every little thing—cares and
joys alike—with heaven on the horizon. What does that look like?

GIFT

Look back and see your memories. Where did you get a glimpse of heaven?
Thank someone for his or her part in that memory.

GRATITUDE

Thank you, Lord, for these blessings:

PRAY THE ROSARY

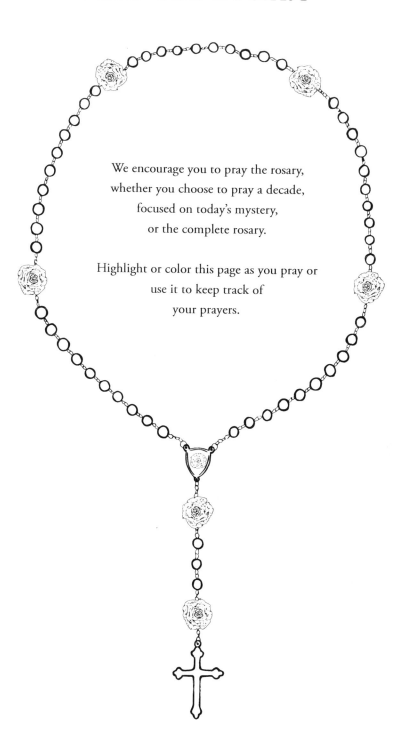

We encourage you to pray the rosary,
whether you choose to pray a decade,
focused on today's mystery,
or the complete rosary.

Highlight or color this page as you pray or
use it to keep track of
your prayers.

LUKE 2:41-52

Now every year his parents went to Jerusalem for the festival of the Passover. And when he was twelve years old, they went up as usual for the festival. When the festival was ended and they started to return, the boy Jesus stayed behind in Jerusalem, but his parents did not know it. Assuming that he was in the group of travelers, they went a day's journey. Then they started to look for him among their relatives and friends. When they did not find him, they returned to Jerusalem to search for him. After three days they found him in the temple, sitting among the teachers, listening to them and asking them questions. And all who heard him were amazed at his understanding and his answers. When his parents saw him they were astonished; and his mother said to him, "Child, why have you treated us like this? Look, your father and I have been searching for you in great anxiety." He said to them, "Why were you searching for me? Did you not know that I must be in my Father's house?" But they did not understand what he said to them. Then he went down with them and came to Nazareth, and was obedient to them. His mother treasured all these things in her heart.
And Jesus increased in wisdom and in years, and in divine and human favor.

TO PONDER: James 3:17

LECTIO DIVINA

THE FINDING IN THE TEMPLE | LUKE 2:41-52

Even at the age of twelve, Jesus knows and understands His identity as the Son of God, and His mission to redeem humanity. Nothing keeps Him from doing the Father's will—not even frightening His parents with his absence! His parents don't fully understand His mission, but they accept it with faith. As in Luke 2:18, Mary continues to ponder these things in her heart.

LECTIO

MEDITATIO

What personal message does the text have for me?

ORATIO

What do I say to the Lord in response to His word?

CONTEMPLATIO

What conversion of mind, heart, and life is He asking of me today?

How did I progress in living the Word today?

THE FIFTH JOYFUL MYSTERY:
THE FINDING IN THE TEMPLE

Last week in an SAT prep lesson, we were studying word choice. "Words are emotionally charged," I explained to my students. I described it through the example of house and home. A house is a structure, a building in which a family might live. A house without a family is still a house, though. A home asks for a certain level of security and emotional warmth. A home needs the family (whatever form that family might take) to truly be a home.

Most people of faith I encounter have a favorite Jesus story in which our Savior does or says something that becomes emblematic of his or her own personal philosophy. The story of Jesus in the temple is that story for me. I am a spatially-driven person. I'm a nester, a lover of hospitality, and a firm believer that we are products of our environments—which is why it is so important for me to live near a church. More specifically, I long to be physically near the tabernacle.

I've been blessed to have lived in two different houses that were so close to church that I could see my living room from my Sunday school classroom. The first of the two was a quirky ranch-style house that I shared with seven of the greatest humans I know. It always smelled of cinnamon and pine. All year, we served each other the best we could, taking turns cooking meals or folding laundry or sitting around the fireplace. It was an interfaith home, where we listened to and respected one another. Our conversations challenged us to grow in our own individual beliefs, as well as to grow in our collective community. As one of my housemates put it, "it was such a healthy place to be a human."

A few years later, I was in search of a place to live for my graduate year. I knew I wanted to be back in that same neighborhood. One of my former housemates saw a yard sign on his way to daily Mass and passed along the contact number. Shortly after, four of my best friends and I had signed for a little white house with a red door. We were a family that year, and we made it a home together. Better yet, the location meant I had both my traditional home and my spiritual home within reach of one another once again.

I vowed not to take for granted the proximity of the adoration chapel. I knew that on long days, taking the extra steps across the street and into the church would give me more peace than walking straight though our red door, our lovable but high-energy friend group sure to be found in the kitchen. And every time I walked the extra few yards, I thought of Jesus in the temple. How badly I want my default to be His house! It's an ongoing effort, though, to maintain the habit of spending time in front of the tabernacle. It requires constant reminders of the importance of being in His presence. The house of my Father is my true home, regardless of where I lay my head at night.

Carly Buckholz

ACTIO

How will I make my life a gift for others in charity?
What does God want me to do today?

GRACE

What is your favorite story; which story of Jesus
is emblematic for you?

GIFT

Give yourself and your Lord the gift of your presence in His Presence.

GRATITUDE

Thank you, Lord, for these blessings:

PRAY THE ROSARY

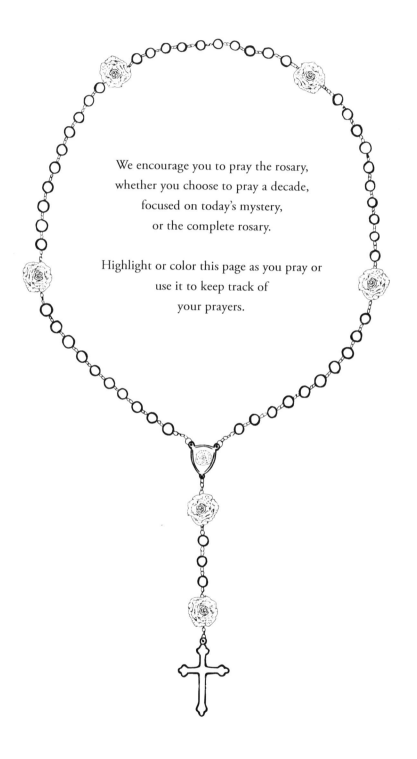

We encourage you to pray the rosary,
whether you choose to pray a decade,
focused on today's mystery,
or the complete rosary.

Highlight or color this page as you pray or
use it to keep track of
your prayers.

Selah

Selah is a Hebrew word found often in the psalms and a few times in Habakkuk. Scholars aren't absolutely certain what it means. It seems to be a musical or liturgical note—maybe a pause or maybe a crescendo.

We have set aside this space—this day—for you to use as your selah. Perhaps you pause here and just review what you have pondered thus far. Perhaps you rejoice here and use the space for shouts of praise. Or maybe you take the opportunity to fill in some gaps in the pages before this one.

It's your space.

Selah.

Give it meaning.

The Joyful Mysteries

Botanical Bouquet

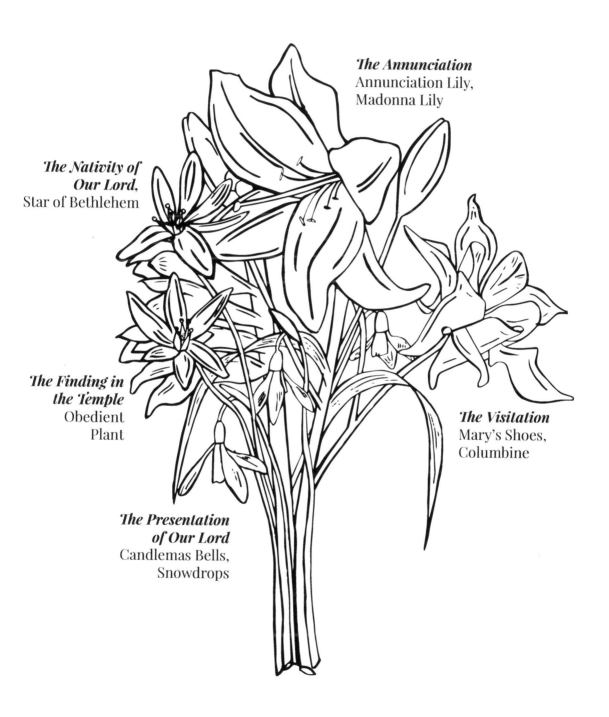

The Annunciation
Annunciation Lily,
Madonna Lily

**The Nativity of
Our Lord,**
Star of Bethlehem

**The Finding in
the Temple**
Obedient
Plant

The Visitation
Mary's Shoes,
Columbine

**The Presentation
of Our Lord**
Candlemas Bells,
Snowdrops

THE

LUMINOUS MYSTERIES

WEEKLY SCRIPTURE MEMORY

THE LUMINOUS MYSTERIES

This week we memorize the moment of movement between Savior and mother before Jesus' first public miracle. Taking Mary's words to heart, we know her instruction is for us, too.

John 2:3-5

When the wine gave out, the mother of Jesus said to him, "They have no wine." And Jesus said to her, "Woman, what concern is that to you and to me? My hour has not yet come."

His mother said to the servants, "Do whatever he tells you."

do whatever He tells you.

JOHN 2:5

DAY NINE

MATTHEW 3:13-17

Then Jesus came from Galilee to John at the Jordan, to be baptized by him. John would have prevented him, saying, "I need to be baptized by you, and do you come to me?" But Jesus answered him, "Let it be so now; for it is proper for us in this way to fulfill all righteousness." Then he consented. And when Jesus had been baptized, just as he came up from the water, suddenly the heavens were opened to him and he saw the Spirit of God descending like a dove and alighting on him. And a voice from heaven said, "This is my Son, the Beloved, with whom I am well pleased."

TO PONDER: Romans 1:7, 1 Corinthians 15:58, James 2:5, Isaiah 62:3, 1 Peter 2:9

LECTIO DIVINA

THE BAPTISM IN THE JORDAN | MATTHEW 3:13-17

The apostle Matthew wrote his Gospel between 50-100 A.D. In it, Matthew carefully shows how the old covenant is fulfilled in the new covenant inaugurated by Christ. This is seen in today's reading; Jesus submits to baptism in order to "fulfill all righteousness." Righteousness, from the Greek *dikaiosune*, indicates the uprightness and faithfulness of God and His people, which God demonstrates through the saving work of Jesus Christ. The new covenant is ratified by Jesus' obedience to the Father.

MEDITATIO

What personal message does the text have for me?

ORATIO

What do I say to the Lord in response to His word?

CONTEMPLATIO

What conversion of mind, heart, and life is He asking of me today?

How did I progress in living the Word today?

THE FIRST LUMINOUS MYSTERY:
THE BAPTISM IN THE JORDAN

Sometimes, I've been grateful to miss a phone call. To someone who cherishes words of affirmation, voicemails are better than a photograph at preserving an intimate memory.

There was that one voicemail from a high school teacher, left after a particularly brutal meeting during a summer journalism conference, reminding me to speak up, because she'd brought me there to be heard. Or that group call from a smattering of friends warning me not to watch a movie because its language would "ruin my innocence." A friend frantically calling from France with sympathy at my father's passing. Mom's traditional, six-second "Hello! It's your mother! Call me back! Bye, love you!"

God the Father doesn't speak too often in the New Testament, but in all three of the Gospel accounts of Jesus' Baptism in the Jordan, God's voice rings in loud and clear, recorded and preserved. When God speaks, He clarifies two things: Jesus' parentage and a Father's pride. "This is my Beloved Son," He says, "with whom I am well pleased" (Matthew 3:17).

Before this, John the Baptist had been faithfully preaching about the One who will baptize with the Holy Spirit and fire, so he is surprised that Jesus asks for his services. Matthew notes that John "would have prevented him," but Jesus basically says, "trust me" (Matthew 3:14). I feel like I've been John a lot lately, reminding God that certain parts of His plan don't make sense. But I love that John asks for clarification, because even if we don't get the answer we want, I don't think God punishes us for asking why. I think He's patient, like He is with John. The result is that everyone present hears a pretty rare phone call from God.

When I'm trying to make a big decision, I wish God could have a family reunion like He does for His Son's Baptism. All three persons are gathered here: the man of the hour, a sign in the form of a dove, and a loud voice from heaven. Usually, in my life,

God chooses to be more subtle, which has the frustrating benefit of making me listen for Him more. But I'm not Jesus and this Baptism isn't subtle at all. This is Jesus' Diana Ross moment—He's beginning His ministry of teaching, preaching, and healing. God the Father is proud.

But here's what I love: Jesus hasn't even begun His public ministry. No miracles, no teachings, no crucifixion. At this point, we know that Jesus has been obedient, a willing participant in the plan. And Jesus is available for whatever God wills. God is well pleased with Him even before the public action of ministry, the things people would applaud. He's proud of Jesus' prep work, proud of His willingness.

He's proud of yours, too.

I work with teenagers, and despite my best efforts, there are few things I can say that will render them speechless. One tactic that always works is when I say I'm proud of them. They usually give me an awkward look and walk away silent—but their shoulders are a little higher, and they work a little harder the next time.

If your parents are still around, do something today that might make them proud. If they are no longer with you, still do the same. If you are a parent, tell your children that you are proud of them. Don't have a big, visible reason—God told his Son that He was proud of Him and He had yet to begin His noteworthy ministry.

My favorite voicemail from my father is just between him and me. But at one point Dad says, "Just so excited, so proud of you; it's just amazing." I still listen to it when I think I've done something worthy of a phone call from him, and pretend he's saying it to me again.

Listen for those messages from your Father, and save them to ponder in your heart.

Katy Greiner

ACTIO

How will I make my life a gift for others in charity?
What does God want me to do today?

GRACE

There are things in your life to which God most certainly has said, "well
done." Did you miss hearing it the first time? Make a list today.
Hear Him now.

GIFT

Notice something good in someone today and speak aloud words of
genuine pride and praise.

GRATITUDE

Thank you, Lord, for these blessings:

PRAY THE ROSARY

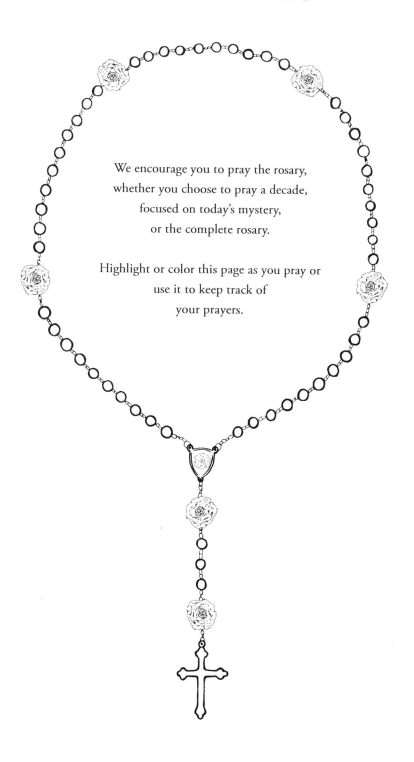

We encourage you to pray the rosary,
whether you choose to pray a decade,
focused on today's mystery,
or the complete rosary.

Highlight or color this page as you pray or
use it to keep track of
your prayers.

JOHN 2:1-11

On the third day there was a wedding in Cana of Galilee, and the mother of Jesus was there. Jesus and his disciples had also been invited to the wedding. When the wine gave out, the mother of Jesus said to him, "They have no wine." And Jesus said to her, "Woman, what concern is that to you and to me? My hour has not yet come." His mother said to the servants, "Do whatever he tells you." Now standing there were six stone water jars for the Jewish rites of purification, each holding twenty or thirty gallons. Jesus said to them, "Fill the jars with water." And they filled them up to the brim. He said to them, "Now draw some out, and take it to the chief steward." So they took it. When the steward tasted the water that had become wine, and did not know where it came from (though the servants who had drawn the water knew), the steward called the bridegroom and said to him, "Everyone serves the good wine first, and then the inferior wine after the guests have become drunk. But you have kept the good wine until now." Jesus did this, the first of his signs, in Cana of Galilee, and revealed his glory; and his disciples believed in him.

TO PONDER: John 12:23-24, Matthew 5:13-16, Romans 13:11-14, Colossians 1:9-14, Acts 13:47

LECTIO DIVINA

THE WEDDING FEAST AT CANA | JOHN 2:1-11

Saint John's Gospel, written before 100 A.D., is the only gospel which contains an account of the wedding at Cana. Mary's simple comment to her Son, motivated by concern for the wedding party, moves Jesus to perform His first public miracle. Her instructions to the steward, "do whatever He tells you", are meant for us as well. We must always do what Jesus tells us.

MEDITATIO

What personal message does the text have for me?

ORATIO

What do I say to the Lord in response to His word?

CONTEMPLATIO

What conversion of mind, heart, and life is He asking of me today?

How did I progress in living the Word today?

THE SECOND LUMINOUS MYSTERY:
THE WEDDING FEAST AT CANA

Her hand was dry and leathery and when she reached for me, my
first reaction was to pull away. Instead, I squeezed her hand in my
own, and I inched closer. I was sixteen or seventeen at the time,
and I was listening to the tragic narrative of a homeless woman
who had AIDS.

We were sitting, knees grazing, in a shelter that ministered to
homeless people who were HIV positive. I remember her hands
were cold, but her smile was warm despite the abject suffering life
had brought her. She recounted how she'd been thrown out of her
home as a teen and had no other option than to sell her body—her
dignity—for money.

One day she decided to make a change and to find a way out. Just
as things were looking up, she found out she had AIDS. She told
her story without bitterness, and she said that she'd found peace.
She'd learned how to live with AIDS, not just die from it.

The memory of that woman made me weep for a long time.
I couldn't get her out of my mind; my heart ached for her. I
remember thinking, not for the first time, why do I have to feel so
much?

More than two decades later, I finally know the answer. Because,
as a woman, I was created to be a conduit of empathy and
compassion. Despite how some might see my female sensitivity
as a liability, it is my most precious gift. As Saint Pope John Paul
II observed, "Perhaps more than men, women acknowledge the
person because they see with their hearts."

I have always loved the wedding feast at Cana (even before I was
married and recognized how it honors the sacredness of marriage).
Christ performs His first miracle here. He changes water into wine
at Mary's request. The moment is imbued with meaning, but what
has always struck me is that Mary sees a need, and she puts in

motion the miracle where her Son fills the need.

"Do whatever he tells you," Mary said at Cana. Her maternal counsel continues today. And here's what Mary's Son is telling you: My beloved, you possess special gifts you are called to bring to the world. You were created to be someone who is inclined to follow the way of the cross, to nurture, and to hold the fabric of society together, not always with high levels of productivity measured in output by hour, but with the gift of self.

We live in a world that is hungry for a woman's gentle touch and compassion. For your gentle touch.

How can we respond as Mary did at Cana?

Our call to love might manifest in the young student who reaches out to a peer on the social margins, or in the health provider who treats the patient and not just the disease. Love takes root in the scared but courageous woman who says yes to the new life growing inside of her despite everyone telling her she has other "choices." It also comes alive in the woman, sitting in a waiting room full of people tethered to smartphones, who puts hers down long enough to look into the eyes of a stranger and smile. It blossoms in the female executive who bravely points out the human cost of corporate decisions. When I was a teen, my heart ached for the homeless woman, so I sat with her and held her hand. Today my heart aches for my crying baby, so I respond to him even if it's in the middle of the night. This is the Mary in all of us coming to life.

Like Mary at Cana, we're charged with connecting others to Jesus. The wedding feast is the second luminous mystery. Be the light, dear sister. There are needs we can fill. Open your eyes and your heart, and do whatever He tells you.

Kate Wicker

ACTIO

How will I make my life a gift for others in charity?
What does God want me to do today?

GRACE

When you are still and quiet, what is the one need He brings to mind today?
Where is the one place He calls you and asks you to do what
He is telling you?

GIFT

Is there a hand you can hold and a gaze you can meet, being steady,
despite wanting to pull away?

GRATITUDE

Thank you, Lord, for these blessings:

PRAY THE ROSARY

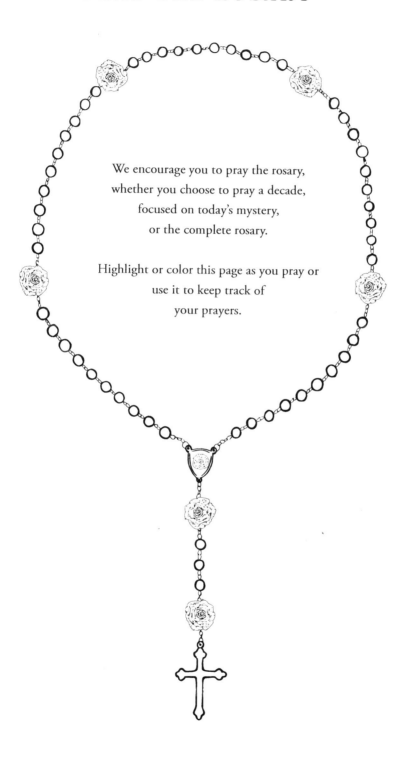

We encourage you to pray the rosary,
whether you choose to pray a decade,
focused on today's mystery,
or the complete rosary.

Highlight or color this page as you pray or
use it to keep track of
your prayers.

MATTHEW 5:1-12

When Jesus saw the crowds, he went up the mountain; and after he sat
down, his disciples came to him. Then he began to speak, and taught
them, saying:

"Blessed are the poor in spirit, for theirs is the kingdom of heaven.

"Blessed are those who mourn, for they will be comforted.

"Blessed are the meek, for they will inherit the earth.

"Blessed are those who hunger and thirst for righteousness, for they will
be filled.

"Blessed are the merciful, for they will receive mercy.

"Blessed are the pure in heart, for they will see God.

"Blessed are the peacemakers, for they will be called children of God.

"Blessed are those who are persecuted for righteousness' sake, for theirs is
the kingdom of heaven.

"Blessed are you when people revile you and persecute you and utter all
kinds of evil against you falsely on my account. Rejoice and be glad, for
your reward is great in heaven, for in the same way they persecuted the
prophets who were before you."

TO PONDER: Matthew 6:9-13, John 15

LECTIO DIVINA

LECTIO

THE PREACHING OF THE KINGDOM | MATTHEW 5:1-12

Today's verses are taken from the Sermon on the Mount, specifically Jesus' teaching of the Beatitudes (which means "state of utmost bliss or happiness"). At heart, the Beatitudes are a portrait of Jesus—He demonstrates each one of these for us, and by doing so, invites us to follow Him, not only in prayer and humility, but in self-sacrifice and hardship.

MEDITATIO

What personal message does the text have for me?

ORATIO

What do I say to the Lord in response to His word?

CONTEMPLATIO

What conversion of mind, heart, and life is He asking of me today?

How did I progress in living the Word today?

THE THIRD LUMINOUS MYSTERY:
THE PREACHING OF THE KINGDOM

Jesus has been preparing for His mission for thirty years. Finally, it's time to tell everyone about His mission, the reason for the incarnation:

"For God so loved the world that he gave his only Son, so that everyone who believes in him may not perish but may have eternal life. Indeed, God did not send the Son into the world to condemn the world, but in order that the world might be saved through him." (John 3:16-17)

In the '90s, that gospel verse seemed to be displayed on poster board at every televised sporting event. At some point during an NFL game, the camera would pan to someone holding a big sign with JOHN 3:16 in thick black Sharpie strokes. It was ubiquitous. At the same time, the WWJD? (What Would Jesus Do) bracelets were a fad at my high school. Everyone seemed to wear one, or have a sticker with the letters on her car, or her locker, or her French class binder.

Upon seeing these stickers, one of my friends remarked, "If we're asking what would Jesus do, then turning over tables is an approved option." We laughed at that, but it's a reminder: publicly approved and sanctioned Christianity can be watered-down, easy Christianity. It can seem like all we have to do is assent to God, believe in Jesus, get baptized, and then we're done. That's it.

In preaching the kingdom, Jesus is constantly calling us to conversion. It's not a one and done moment. Every moment of our lives, we have to be converting, becoming more like Jesus. That is not easy. The Beatitudes, which we are reading today, are at the center of the gospel. They outline the vocation of a Christian and illustrate how to live an authentic

Christian life. They are, most assuredly, not easy.

Jesus asks us to be poor in spirit. To mourn over our sins. To be meek. To hunger and thirst for righteousness. To be merciful. To be pure in heart. To be peacemakers. And, to top it off, He tells us that when we are persecuted (not if, but when), we should be happy about it.

Is Jesus crazy? Who in her right mind would sign up for this? Who feels at all able to live this life? I know I don't.

For example: I'm not meek. I'm Italian. And Scots-Irish. And German. There is nothing in that ethnic makeup that makes being meek easy. Whenever I hear verses about being meek and humble of heart, I cringe, because I really don't know how to do that. I haven't learned how to be gentle but strong. It's going to be a lifelong lesson for me.

Maybe you feel that way, too. Maybe it's not a verse in the Beatitudes, but somewhere else in the gospel, that touches you in a tender place. You think that you cannot do what Jesus is asking. It's just too hard.

It is hard. And Jesus knows just how hard it is: "For we do not have a high priest who is unable to sympathize with our weaknesses, but we have one who in every respect has been tested as we are, yet without sin. Let us therefore approach the throne of grace with boldness, so that we may receive mercy and find grace to help in time of need." (Hebrews 4:15-16)

When you have trouble, go to Jesus. He will give you the mercy and grace you need to persevere. His yoke is easy, and His burden is light. (Matthew 11:30) Trust Him in that. Then pick yourself up, dust yourself off, and go preach the kingdom with Jesus.

Emily DeArdo

ACTIO

How will I make my life a gift for others in charity?
What does God want me to do today?

GRACE

What's a Beatitude you struggle with? Why is this one in particular such a
struggle? What are some ways you could focus on bringing that into your life
the way Christ did?

GIFT

Take a moment to thoughtfully thank someone who teaches today.

GRATITUDE

Thank you, Lord, for these blessings:

PRAY THE ROSARY

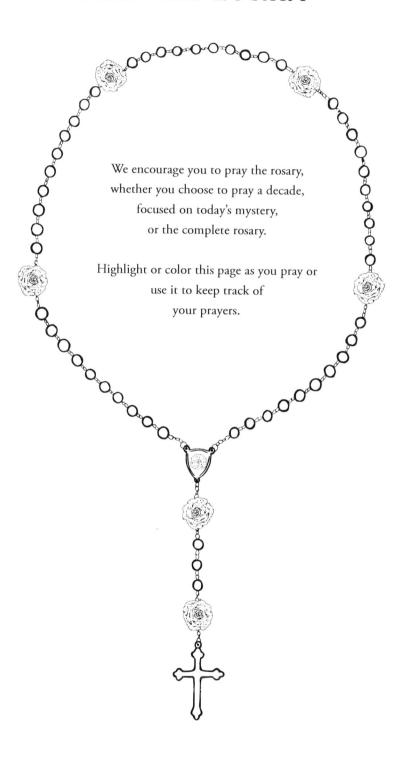

We encourage you to pray the rosary,
whether you choose to pray a decade,
focused on today's mystery,
or the complete rosary.

Highlight or color this page as you pray or
use it to keep track of
your prayers.

LUKE 9:28-36

Now about eight days after these sayings Jesus took with him Peter and John and James, and went up on the mountain to pray. And while he was praying, the appearance of his face changed, and his clothes became dazzling white. Suddenly they saw two men, Moses and Elijah, talking to him. They appeared in glory and were speaking of his departure, which he was about to accomplish at Jerusalem. Now Peter and his companions were weighed down with sleep; but since they had stayed awake, they saw his glory and the two men who stood with him. Just as they were leaving him, Peter said to Jesus, "Master, it is good for us to be here; let us make three dwellings, one for you, one for Moses, and one for Elijah"—not knowing what he said. While he was saying this, a cloud came and overshadowed them; and they were terrified as they entered the cloud. Then from the cloud came a voice that said, "This is my Son, my Chosen; listen to him!" When the voice had spoken, Jesus was found alone. And they kept silent and in those days told no one any of the things they had seen.

TO PONDER: Exodus 3, 1 Kings 19:11-13

LECTIO DIVINA

THE TRANSFIGURATION | LUKE 9:28-36

The Transfiguration allows Jesus' closest disciples to see Him in glory as Jesus manifests Himself truly to them, which strengthens their faith. It also affirms Christ's fulfillment of the Law and the prophets by showing Him with Moses, the lawgiver, and Elijah, the greatest of the Old Testament prophets. The voice of the Father, the presence of Jesus the Son, and the cloud of the Holy Spirit also manifest the Blessed Trinity, as also occurred at Jesus' baptism.

MEDITATIO

What personal message does the text have for me?

ORATIO

What do I say to the Lord in response to His word?

CONTEMPLATIO

What conversion of mind, heart, and life is He asking of me today?

How did I progress in living the Word today?

THE FOURTH LUMINOUS MYSTERY:
THE TRANSFIGURATION

As I write this devotion, I am preparing again to accompany 150 high school students to a remote campground for our parish's annual youth ministry winter retreat. The thought of spending a weekend isolated with so many young people is enough to drive anyone to pick up their rosary and beg our Lady for assistance.

What is it about leaving the valley and going up a mountain that inspires teenagers to give up their phones, their friends, and their comfy beds for an entire weekend? I think it's the same thing that inspired Jesus to bring Peter, James, and John up the mountain: an encounter with the living God.

Imagine you're standing next to Peter on top of a beautiful mountain, and Jesus is transfigured a few feet away. Not only does His garment become whiter than snow, but He reveals Himself in a whole new way to the disciples who love Him most. In the midst of this experience, they hear the voice of God say, "This is my Beloved Son. Listen to Him."

Listen to Him.

I know how hard it is for me to hear God's voice amidst the chaos and noise of daily life, and most teenagers today face even more obstacles. So away to the mountaintop we go, seeking a transformative experience with Jesus.

One of my favorite moments of the retreat is Adoration on Saturday night. At this point, the kids have been challenged to walk with purpose, to live out their Christian lives with intention and passion. They've experienced healing and the restoration of their souls in the Sacrament of Confession. Then they come face to face with Jesus in the monstrance during Adoration. It is in this moment that everything changes. Sometimes there are tears. Sometimes there is laughter. Sometimes there is shock when they realize they are face to face with the living God. I imagine that Peter, James, and John reacted in a similar way when Jesus revealed His Mystical Body to them.

One cannot remain unchanged after this encounter. It's just not possible. If we are open to receiving whatever the Lord has for us, He will transform us. Isn't this what we all desire? To be transformed into a better version of ourselves? To be able to serve with joy and meet people right where they are, bringing them the light of Christ's love and His healing mercy?

On Sunday, when we leave the mountain and return to the valley, the spiritual change is evident in their countenances and their behavior. The challenge is to keep that change in their hearts so it can pour forth into their lives. We are asked to bring the lessons learned on the mountaintop into the valley of our daily experience. But how do we accomplish this?

The key is not to let go of that holy gaze. When we keep our eyes fixed on Christ and our hearts solidly in the present moment, than we can allow God to transform us from the inside out.

As you meditate on this beautiful mystery of the rosary, take yourself to that mountaintop with the disciples. Put yourself in front of Jesus as He reveals the beauty of His eternal nature to you. Soak it in like rain on parched land. Allow Him to fill the crevices of your heart and mind with beauty and truth. Listen as He whispers blessings upon you. Then go forth and live as He has instructed you to, with courage and faith.

Mary Lenaburg

ACTIO

How will I make my life a gift for others in charity?
What does God want me to do today?

GRACE

We can't always experience God on retreat at the top of a mountain. Today,
where can you find that moment to behold His glory in
your everyday world?

GIFT

Go out of your way to find someone whose native language is different from
your own. Communicate in a meaningful way. Transcend the difference.
Smile warmly, and shine with the luminous glory of God.

GRATITUDE

Thank you, Lord, for these blessings:

PRAY THE ROSARY

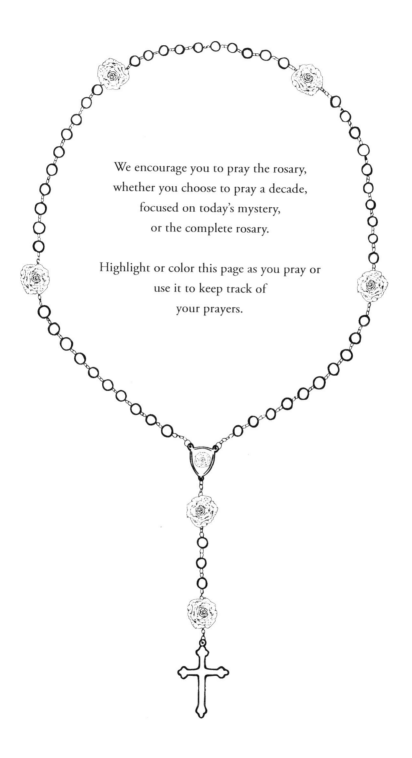

We encourage you to pray the rosary,
whether you choose to pray a decade,
focused on today's mystery,
or the complete rosary.

Highlight or color this page as you pray or
use it to keep track of
your prayers.

MATTHEW 26:26-29

While they were eating, Jesus took a loaf of bread, and after blessing it he broke it, gave it to the disciples, and said, "Take, eat; this is my body." Then he took a cup, and after giving thanks he gave it to them, saying, "Drink from it, all of you; for this is my blood of the covenant, which is poured out for many for the forgiveness of sins. I tell you, I will never again drink of this fruit of the vine until that day when I drink it new with you in my Father's kingdom."

JOHN 6:53-56

So Jesus said to them, "Very truly, I tell you, unless you eat the flesh of the Son of Man and drink his blood, you have no life in you. Those who eat my flesh and drink my blood have eternal life, and I will raise them up on the last day; for my flesh is true food and my blood is true drink. Those who eat my flesh and drink my blood abide in me, and I in them."

TO PONDER: Mark 14:22-25, Luke 22:17-19, 1 Corinthians 10:16, 1 Corinthians 11:23-26, Matthew 14:19, Hebrews 9:20, Exodus 24:6-8

LECTIO DIVINA

THE INSTITUTION OF THE EUCHARIST | MATTHEW 26:26-29

The night before His death, Jesus shares the Passover meal with His apostles. Jesus takes bread and wine and uses them to institute the Sacrament of the Eucharist. At Mass, the priest repeats Jesus' words as he consecrates the bread and wine, which become the Body and Blood of the Lord through the miracle of transubstantiation. Jesus is truly present—body, blood, soul, and divinity—at every Mass. The Eucharist is the source and summit of the Christian life (CCC 1324).

MEDITATIO

What personal message does the text have for me?

ORATIO

What do I say to the Lord in response to His word?

CONTEMPLATIO

What conversion of mind, heart, and life is He asking of me today?

How did I progress in living the Word today?

THE FIFTH LUMINOUS MYSTERY:
THE INSTITUTION OF THE EUCHARIST

Looking back on my Protestant upbringing, communion Sundays are a fond childhood memory: the solemn passing of the trays, taking dainty bites of the wafer and delicate sips of sweet grape juice, wanting to make them last for as long as I could. I knew I was supposed to be thinking about Jesus. My mom told me that this was a symbol of His sacrifice. And somehow these tiny morsels were intended to remind me of Him and the fact that He had given His life for me, but I'm afraid I was more enamored of the small portions, with making a game as children so often do. After all, this was simply a symbolic ritual we participated in on occasion—it wasn't our Daily Bread.

Imagine my surprise when, years later, I encountered Catholic teaching on the Real Presence of Jesus in the Eucharist in a handful of books a Catholic friend loaned me. The idea that the Last Supper was much more than a final meal shared by Jesus and His friends, more than a painting on the wall, was absolutely foreign to me. That happy ritual from my childhood was meant to be more than a symbol, more than a rare sip of grape juice. This was Jesus giving himself, flesh and blood, to all of us.

I spent hours poring through books on Catholic teaching alongside my Bible, and I read Jesus' words with new eyes. "Truly, truly, I say to you, unless you eat the flesh of the Son of man and drink His blood, you have no life in you." (John 6:53)

I read His words over and over again.

"For my flesh is food indeed, and my blood is drink indeed. He who eats my flesh and drinks my blood abides in me, and I in him." (John 6:55-56)

That fall, I entered into the process of learning the Catholic faith and progressing towards converting, full of both hope and trepidation. Being raised in a family that was vehemently opposed to Catholicism, I was afraid of what my parents were going to say. But I couldn't deny what I believed because of fear. And I wanted this most precious gift; I wanted so much to receive Jesus in the Eucharist. I had spent most of my life searching for the truth, for the message that would transform me, that would set me free. And all along, Jesus was there. It was His Body and His Blood that would truly transform and sanctify me. More than a decade after my joyous entry into the Catholic Church, there is no doubt that I am a new person, fed by His Body, His Blood, and the very real grace with which He fills me.

Still, there is a temptation to stay home some days, to take the gift for granted—too tired, too overwhelmed by the very blessings (eight children!) that are fruits of my Catholic faith. But even on those Sundays when I don't feel up to leaving the house, I go, because I know He's waiting for me there, and I know I need Him.

When Jesus promised, "I am with you always, to the close of the age" (Matthew 28:20), He meant He would be with us not only on a mystical level, but also in this gloriously tangible way, in the Eucharist. Friends, we must not forget how precious this gift is. Jesus is here with us and in us always. Never let the mystery and the majesty, the awe of it, fade. This is Jesus becoming part of me, part of you, transforming us all for His glory.

Ginny Sheller

ACTIO

How will I make my life a gift for others in charity?
What does God want me to do today?

GRACE

In what moments is God most real in your life? How can you be more
available for those moments?

GIFT

Grateful for the gift of the Eucharist, add an extra Mass to
your calendar this week.

GRATITUDE

Thank you, Lord, for these blessings:

PRAY THE ROSARY

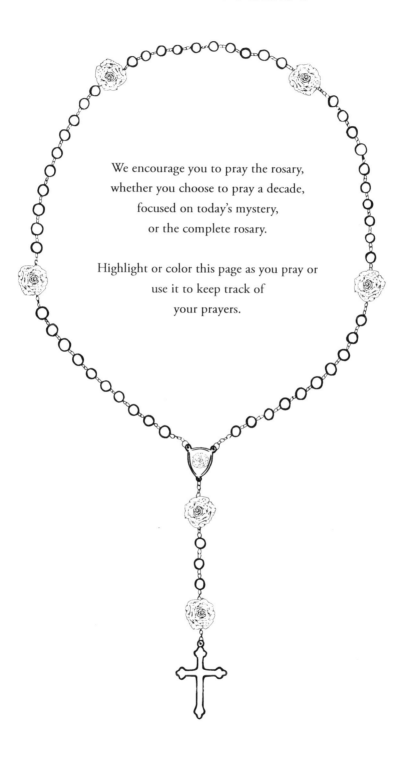

We encourage you to pray the rosary,
whether you choose to pray a decade,
focused on today's mystery,
or the complete rosary.

Highlight or color this page as you pray or
use it to keep track of
your prayers.

Selah

DAY FOURTEEN

Selah is a Hebrew word found often in the psalms and a few times in Habakkuk. Scholars aren't absolutely certain what it means. It seems to be a musical or liturgical note—maybe a pause or maybe a crescendo.

We have set aside this space—this day—for you to use as your selah. Perhaps you pause here and just review what you have pondered thus far. Perhaps you rejoice here and use the space for shouts of praise. Or maybe you take the opportunity to fill in some gaps in the pages before this one.

It's your space.

Selah.

Give it meaning.

The Luminous Mysteries

Botanical Bouquet

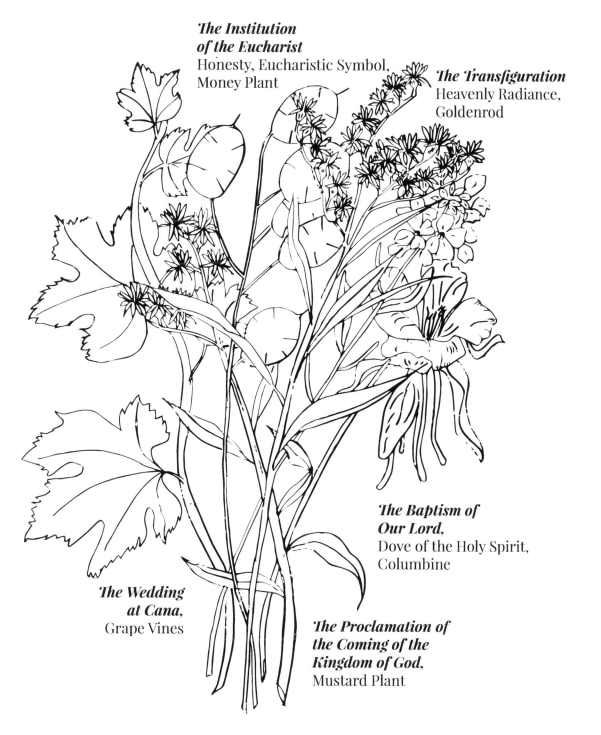

**The Institution
of the Eucharist**
Honesty, Eucharistic Symbol,
Money Plant

The Transfiguration
Heavenly Radiance,
Goldenrod

**The Baptism of
Our Lord,**
Dove of the Holy Spirit,
Columbine

**The Wedding
at Cana,**
Grape Vines

**The Proclamation of
the Coming of the
Kingdom of God,**
Mustard Plant

THE

SORROWFUL MYSTERIES

WEEKLY SCRIPTURE MEMORY

THE SORROWFUL MYSTERIES

As we allow ourselves to walk with Jesus on the road to Calvary and to hang with Jesus on the cross, let's bury these words deep inside of us so that we can be of one mind with the Savior.

Philippians 2:4-8

Let each of you look not to your own interests, but to the interests of others. Let the same mind be in you that was in Christ Jesus,
who, though he was in the form of God,
    did not regard equality with God
    as something to be exploited,
 but emptied himself,
    taking the form of a slave,
    being born in human likeness.
And being found in human form,
  he humbled himself
    and became obedient to the point of death—
    even death on a cross.

let the
same mind
be in you
that was
in
Christ
Jesus.

PHILIPPIANS 2:5

LUKE 22:39-46

He came out and went, as was his custom, to the Mount of Olives; and the disciples followed him. When he reached the place, he said to them, "Pray that you may not come into the time of trial." Then he withdrew from them about a stone's throw, knelt down, and prayed, "Father, if you are willing, remove this cup from me; yet, not my will but yours be done." [[Then an angel from heaven appeared to him and gave him strength. In his anguish he prayed more earnestly, and his sweat became like great drops of blood falling down on the ground.]] When he got up from prayer, he came to the disciples and found them sleeping because of grief, and he said to them, "Why are you sleeping? Get up and pray that you may not come into the time of trial."

TO PONDER: Hebrews 2:5-11, 1 Peter 2:18-25, 1 Peter 5:10

LECTIO DIVINA

THE AGONY IN THE GARDEN | LUKE 22:39-46

Saint Luke was a medical doctor, and this led him to focus on Jesus' humanity throughout his gospel. This excerpt gives us a vivid example of that humanity; sweating blood (called hematidrosis) only occurs under conditions of extreme physical and mental stress. Even though He is God, Jesus is also man, and His fear, stress, and anxiety are powerfully presented here. Nevertheless, Jesus accepts His Father's plan.

MEDITATIO

What personal message does the text have for me?

ORATIO

What do I say to the Lord in response to His word?

CONTEMPLATIO

What conversion of mind, heart, and life is He asking of me today?

How did I progress in living the Word today?

THE FIRST SORROWFUL MYSTERY:
THE AGONY IN THE GARDEN

This mystery is one of my favorites. I know that sounds odd. Jesus, the night before He dies, is in the midst of terrible mental and physical suffering. He knows what's going to happen to Him over the next few hours: the physical torture, the mockery, the humiliation. And, like every other human being, He's afraid.

Sometimes we forget the humanity of Jesus. This mystery brings it to the fore.

I've never been asked to save mankind. But I've had many nights where I've cried myself to sleep, begging God to show me that everything was going to turn out OK— that the pain of the present moment was going to be redeemed, and that, eventually, something akin to the resurrection would happen.

When you're twenty-three, and you're dying, you really want to know the plan. At least I did. Night after night, I had to accept—again—and trust—again—in the plan that God had for me. I had been diagnosed with cystic fibrosis twelve years before. Now, the only thing that was going to save me was a double-lung transplant. For me to live, someone else had to die. There were no more drugs, no more medical magic. Just the bald facts: seventeen percent of my lungs worked. I weighed eighty-three pounds. If a set of lungs didn't come in time, I would die.

I didn't sweat blood, like Jesus did in the garden, during my nightly conversations with God. I just cried normal human tears, quietly, so I wouldn't wake up my parents and my siblings, who slept down the hall. But I did beg God to let me know that this was all going to be OK. I wanted to know the end of the story. I wanted a burning bush in my bedroom.

I always knew that Jesus understood how I felt, and that was comforting. He knew the intense mental agony, the fear, the helplessness, the surrender that was required to do God's will. Because it was surrender, when the tears were gone, to say to God, "thy will be done. You are in charge of my life, not me." I'd prayed the "Our Father" since I was a child, and "thy will be done" is part of the prayer. But I just sort of sped over that part. Yeah, yeah, thy will be done. Now, though—now I knew that God's will *would* be done. And the easiest way forward was to surrender to that, to give up my imperfect ideas, for the perfection of His plan. I'm an ESTJ, the "executive" of personality types. I like to control things. Surrendering my will is antithetical to me.

But God was asking me to literally lay my life in His hands. I had to constantly, unceasingly, give up my will to God, because He was the only way out of the darkness.

In the agony in the garden, Jesus shares our suffering. He knows how much we fight against God's will. And He shows us, as He always does, the way forward. Even when the way forward is terrifying, and not want we want, and we scream, and we would write the story differently. But then, that story wouldn't be the one God wants to write.

He writes our stories so precisely, calculates the crosses perfectly to our strength. But that doesn't mean that the cross is easy. Because it's not. The cross is often terrifying. But the story's ending, if we stick with it, is glorious. The cross is the only way home.

Emily DeArdo

ACTIO

How will I make my life a gift for others in charity?
What does God want me to do today?

GRACE

Think of a time when you wanted to know the end of a story because you were afraid. How did God eventually write the conclusion to that chapter?

GIFT

Look for the suffering today. Take a deep breath, offer a silent prayer for strength and grace, then sit with someone who is hurting and offer the gift of your presence.

GRATITUDE

Thank you, Lord, for these blessings:

PRAY THE ROSARY

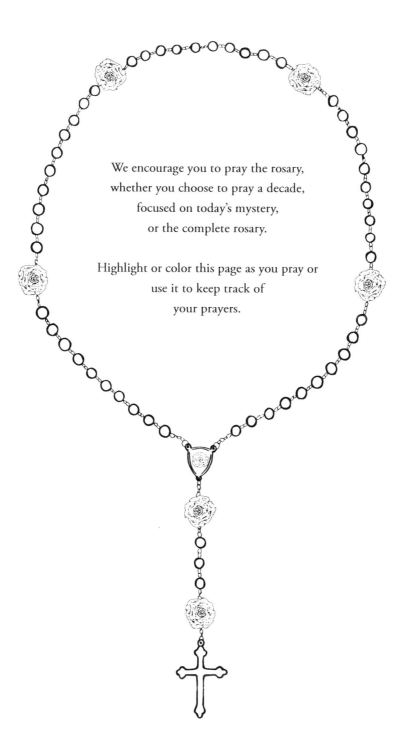

We encourage you to pray the rosary,
whether you choose to pray a decade,
focused on today's mystery,
or the complete rosary.

Highlight or color this page as you pray or
use it to keep track of
your prayers.

JOHN 19:1

Then Pilate took Jesus and had him flogged.

ISAIAH 53:4-5

Surely he has borne our infirmities
   and carried our diseases;
yet we accounted him stricken,
   struck down by God, and afflicted.

But he was wounded for our transgressions,
   crushed for our iniquities;
upon him was the punishment that made us whole,
   and by his bruises we are healed.

TO PONDER: Psalm 22

LECTIO DIVINA

LECTIO

THE SCOURGING AT THE PILLAR | JOHN 19:1

Scourging, or flogging, was a prelude to crucifixion under the Romans, and was also used as punishment for the worst criminals and rebellious slaves. Jesus was tied to a pillar, and then lashed with leather whips that had pieces of metal or bone attached to the ends, in order to tear the skin. Flagellation could be fatal, due to the severity of the injuries incurred.

MEDITATIO

What personal message does the text have for me?

ORATIO

What do I say to the Lord in response to His word?

CONTEMPLATIO

What conversion of mind, heart, and life is He asking of me today?

How did I progress in living the Word today?

THE SECOND SORROWFUL MYSTERY:
THE SCOURGING AT THE PILLAR

It is opening night. The movie doesn't begin for another ninety minutes, yet a large crowd has already gathered, eager to stream into the run-down building and claim a seat in the cramped theater.

Eventually the lights go down and the projector flickers on. I don't realize in that moment, but my relationship with Jesus will never be the same.

I know the story of Christ's Passion as well as I know my own family's history. I've heard it told and re-told each Lenten season since I was a child. And yet. There is something about seeing the words of the evangelists portrayed on the big screen that makes it more realistic than it has ever been.

Soon enough, the crowds are shouting, "Crucify Him!" demanding that Pontius Pilate exact justice for Jesus' blasphemy. A shiver runs down my spine as I recall the countless times I have proclaimed those same words during the Passion at Mass: "Crucify Him!" Pilate, finding no wrongdoing with Jesus, nevertheless feels compelled to placate the angry mob, and sentences Him to be scourged. Surely, once He is beaten, the crowd will be pacified. And so, "… Pilate took Jesus and had him flogged" (John 19:1).

As our Lord is dragged to the pillar, I wince. I know that things are about to get real. Too real. Jesus is whipped—again and again and yet again. His eyes roll back in His sacred head from pain. The air is knocked from His lungs by the guards' savagery. His punishment is like sport for His torturers—they compete to see who will strike the blow that elicits cries for mercy from their prisoner. And yet no cry comes.

His precious blood spills to the ground, His flesh is ripped from His bones, His legs buckle under the force of the countless attacks on His battered body. The guards grow weary, having exhausted themselves with the physical effort of breaking Him.

And yet He bears these tortures with meekness. With humility. With unimaginable love.

Sitting on the edge of my seat, reality sets in. The profundity of this moment causes the scales to fall from my eyes. I recognize that it is not just the crowd or the government who has condemned Jesus to suffer.

I am reminded of a not-too-distant past when I lived a life of my own design, one of bondage to worldly comforts and values. One where I believed freedom meant license to do whatever I wanted regardless the laws of God. One where Jesus Christ was merely a nice idea and not the unequivocal King of my heart.

In this dark movie theater, my soul is laid bare. I am face to face with the consequence of my sin—past, present, and future—this spotless victim, this saving victim, beaten almost beyond recognition at the bloody pillar. Hot tears of shame and regret stream down my cheeks.

Oh, Jesus. My Jesus. I did this to you. Me. My sin.

Crucify Him.

These images of Our Lord—bruised, bloodied, and broken—are forever seared into my soul. It's something that I cannot erase, cannot unsee. As painful and difficult and gruesome as these images are, I am grateful for them. They come to mind every time I pray the sorrowful mysteries of the rosary. And they come to mind nearly every time I am tempted to sin.

These images remind me that He loves me so much that He bore the wounds of every single one of my transgressions. My sins. I am not worthy of such a love, of such mercy, such grace and forgiveness. Yet He offers it to me, willingly. Freely. And by His stripes, I am healed.

Heather Renshaw

ACTIO

How will I make my life a gift for others in charity?
What does God want me to do today?

GRACE

Have you seen *The Passion of the Christ*? What images stand out to you? Have
you avoided it? Is it time to watch and not look away?

GIFT

Offer yourself today to someone with a physical need: a shut-in, a new mom,
a nursing home resident, a sick friend. Or, offer respite to someone who is a
full-time caregiver to someone with exceptional physical needs.

GRATITUDE

Thank you, Lord, for these blessings:

PRAY THE ROSARY

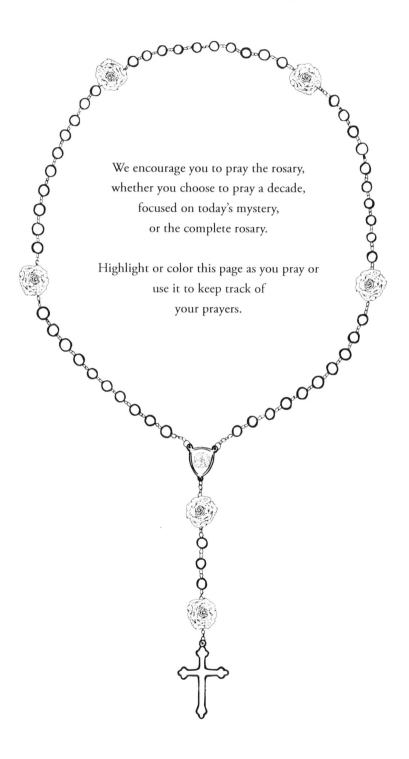

We encourage you to pray the rosary,
whether you choose to pray a decade,
focused on today's mystery,
or the complete rosary.

Highlight or color this page as you pray or
use it to keep track of
your prayers.

MATTHEW 27:27-31

Then the soldiers of the governor took Jesus into the governor's headquarters, and they gathered the whole cohort around him. They stripped him and put a scarlet robe on him, and after twisting some thorns into a crown, they put it on his head. They put a reed in his right hand and knelt before him and mocked him, saying, "Hail, King of the Jews!" They spat on him, and took the reed and struck him on the head. After mocking him, they stripped him of the robe and put his own clothes on him. Then they led him away to crucify him.

TO PONDER: Mark 15:16-20, John 19:2

LECTIO DIVINA

LECTIO

Jesus has been scourged, but that is not enough for the people. They demand that He be crucified, and Pilate, afraid that the crowd will riot, gives into their demands. But first, Jesus endures more pain, both physical and emotional: He is mocked, beaten, spat upon, and crowned with thorns. The thorns would have been about three to four inches long, causing intense physical pain as they tore into Jesus' flesh.

MEDITATIO

What personal message does the text have for me?

ORATIO

What do I say to the Lord in response to His word?

CONTEMPLATIO

What conversion of mind, heart, and life is He asking of me today?

How did I progress in living the Word today?

THE THIRD SORROWFUL MYSTERY:
THE CROWNING WITH THORNS

When I was growing up, I had the hardest time repeating the words, "Crucify Him!" on Good Friday. You'd think I'd relish the opportunity to shout in a church, but those words—they never felt right coming out of my mouth. Even at a young age, I pitied those first century Jews and Romans. How foolish they were. How lacking in grace. How utterly unlike me.

"Present-day Jews must feel so awful about their ancestors crucifying Jesus," I remember mentioning to my mom. I'll never forget the horrified look on her face. Sternly, and without hesitation, she rebuked me.

"Micaela, you and I are as guilty of Christ's death as those Pharisees and those Romans."

Oh, pride. You are every thorn in the tragically precious crown of my Lord.

In 1925, Pope Pius XI established the Feast of Christ the King. His encyclical, *Quas Primas*, delineates the nature of the Kingship of Christ. Jesus should, he said, reign in our minds, our wills, our hearts, and our bodies, and He should be the Master of both our public and private lives.

Following the great pope's wisdom, then, we should think of Christ, conform our wills to His, love Him dearly, and carry out His commands on earth. In essence, Christ should govern every aspect of our human nature.

For us independent Americans, servitude is a tough pill to swallow. We love our democracy, and the fact that we choose our leaders. They serve us and our needs, not the other way around. Which is all well and good for humanity, but what about our Divine Master?

Pope Pius XI also encourages us to acknowledge Christ's lordship over the whole world. The relationship isn't simply a private love between a Father and a child (although we certainly should love Him and speak to Him as a daughter would) but also one of a subject to her king. Indeed, not just our own personal king, but King of the whole wide world, whether they acknowledge Him or not. As faithful followers, we should neither be ashamed to be His servants, nor reticent to share our love for Him.

Which brings us back to that praetorium. Before the eyes of the whole wide world—Jews and Gentiles—Jesus was mocked. They stripped Him, clothed Him in royal garb, bestowed a crown of thorns upon His precious head, and finally, jeering at Him, they bowed before Him in a caricature of homage.

They rejected Jesus Christ as the King of their minds, wills, hearts, and bodies. How very foolish and unlike us… right?

Oh, friends. It's so uncomplicated to see the sins of others, to look at atheists, heretics, even other Catholic Christians and judge them. They must not know the Truth. They must not love Christ like I do. They must not have Him as the King of their lives.

This, my friends, is why I love the third sorrowful mystery so very much. Even as my pride wants to take credit for how much I love and deserve love from Jesus, my heart knows that I crown Him with thorns a thousand times a day. I crown Him every time I choose my own way instead of His, every time I profess to love others but privately follow the way of selfishness, every time I seek glory for myself instead of offering it to Him.

How will we love and serve our King today? Will we crown Him with thorns as the Pharisees and the Gentiles did, mocking Him? Or will we crown Him with gold and jewels as Pope Pius XI encourages us to, publicly and privately, with our mind, will, heart, and body?

Lord, let me crown You with gold and not with thorns. Let my fealty to You be true and unwavering.

Micaela Darr

ACTIO

How will I make my life a gift for others in charity?
What does God want me to do today?

GRACE

What is one tangible way you can replace a crown of thorns with a crown of
gold today?

GIFT

Speak light and life into someone who feels discouraged and overlooked.

GRATITUDE

Thank you, Lord, for these blessings:

PRAY THE ROSARY

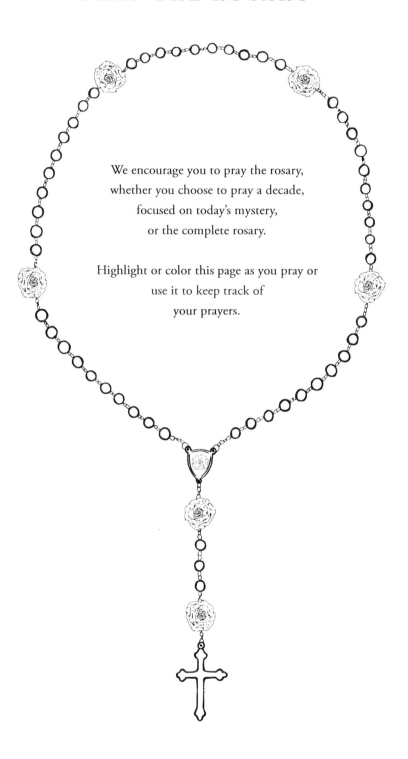

We encourage you to pray the rosary,
whether you choose to pray a decade,
focused on today's mystery,
or the complete rosary.

Highlight or color this page as you pray or
use it to keep track of
your prayers.

LUKE 23:26-31

As they led him away, they seized a man, Simon of Cyrene, who was coming from the country, and they laid the cross on him, and made him carry it behind Jesus. A great number of the people followed him, and among them were women who were beating their breasts and wailing for him. But Jesus turned to them and said, "Daughters of Jerusalem, do not weep for me, but weep for yourselves and for your children. For the days are surely coming when they will say, 'Blessed are the barren, and the wombs that never bore, and the breasts that never nursed.' Then they will begin to say to the mountains, 'Fall on us'; and to the hills, 'Cover us.' For if they do this when the wood is green, what will happen when it is dry?"

TO PONDER: Matthew 27:32-34, Mark 15:20-33, John 19:16-18, Mark 8:31-37, Philippians 4:13

LECTIO DIVINA

THE CARRYING OF THE CROSS | LUKE 23:26-31

In His encounter with the women, Jesus alludes to several Old Testament verses, particularly Hosea 10:8. He prophesies that Jerusalem will taste the bitterness of war and devastation for its prolonged impertinence towards God. By addressing the women as "daughters of Jerusalem," He may be identifying them with the righteous women described by the prophet Ezekiel, who will survive the devastation and become a source of consolation of others.

MEDITATIO

What personal message does the text have for me?

ORATIO

What do I say to the Lord in response to His word?

CONTEMPLATIO

What conversion of mind, heart, and life is He asking of me today?

How did I progress in living the Word today?

THE FOURTH SORROWFUL MYSTERY:
THE CARRYING OF THE CROSS

"You just have to carry your cross." It's a phrase we throw around with a certain spiritual nonchalance at times, as if the reality of pain and suffering is to be expected. The solution is clear and simple: Buck up and carry that cross. After all, that's what Jesus did.

I sit to type these words the morning I will bury my mother. It is the latest in a series of deep pains that have marked my life. I have buried my own tiny son, my father, my brother, my mother-in-law. And now this. I have dragged along the cross of grief for so long that my mental and emotional health have buckled under its weight and now mental illness digs its splinters into my shoulders every time I lean to take the next step. I do not know the full effect this added weight will have on my next steps, or the ones that come years from now, or the last ones I take on the way to my "it is done" moment. What I do know right now is that no amount of simply digging in to get the job done will be enough to cover my wounds and make this weight seem bearable.

But if, for a moment, I look away from the Christian platitudes and the seeming pressure to make this cross-carrying life neat and tidy for everyone else, and I look instead to Jesus, I find a Savior who doesn't bear the burden of His cross with aplomb. He is bruised and broken. The people who love Him are not moved to cheer Him on, but to weep for Him. He is God, on His way to do the very thing He took on human skin to do. Yet He falls repeatedly under the weight of the task. There is nothing neat and tidy about the way Jesus saves us. The carrying of the cross is no easy redemption. It is the reality of our Lord down in the dust with us, bleeding and broken with us, falling and rising with us again and again, and taking that one next step with us. He tests the weight of the cross, and even as the burden of our sin digs deeper into

His already broken heart, our sweet Savior takes that next step, and the next, and the next, all the way to the top of the hill of our salvation.

I am comforted knowing that there is nothing in the heart of my Savior that wants me to pretend that this is easy work, this cross-carrying life. The Scriptures speak over and over again of the Lord's compassion for us. Compassion is derived from roots that give it the meaning "to suffer with." Our God is no bystander cheering us on to buck up under the weight of this life. He is there, looking at us with knowing eyes, extending a scarred hand to us when we fall, wiping our faces when the sweat and tears threaten to blind us, weeping with us even as He sees the glory that awaits us on the other side of our pain.

Perhaps there is another connotation we can use to buoy the well-worn phrase of "carry your cross," instead of encouragement to simply get the job done. If I stop to meditate on the way my Jesus carried His cross, I find a model for carrying my own that teaches me this truth: My salvation comes at a great cost. My Savior bore it as a burden, dragged it up that hill as His human flesh failed Him over and over again. He broke Himself open for me in a million smaller ways before He ever reached that spot where He would die for me. That same Savior watches me bear the ever-growing weight of my own cross with the same heart, a heart that beats and bleeds and breaks for my pain. When He calls out to give me strength, His voice cracks with compassion as He suffers with me. Instead of feeling the pressure to somehow make this walk toward eternity look simple, neat, or easy, I am filled with the knowledge that when I walk with my Savior, I can walk broken-hearted, dirty, weary, and weeping. And He will be there to take the next step with me, all the way until it is done.

Colleen Connell Mitchell

ACTIO

How will I make my life a gift for others in charity?
What does God want me to do today?

GRACE

Who are the people in your life who help you carry your crosses? Make sure
you notice.

GIFT

Help someone today to do a job that is not yours, but his or hers.

GRATITUDE

Thank you, Lord, for these blessings:

DAY NINETEEN

PRAY THE ROSARY

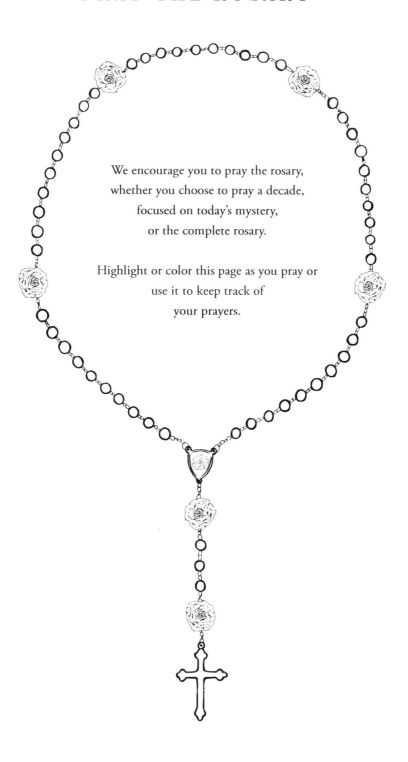

We encourage you to pray the rosary,
whether you choose to pray a decade,
focused on today's mystery,
or the complete rosary.

Highlight or color this page as you pray or
use it to keep track of
your prayers.

DAY TWENTY

MATTHEW 27:35-56

And when they had crucified him, they divided his clothes among themselves by casting lots; then they sat down there and kept watch over him. Over his head they put the charge against him, which read, "This is Jesus, the King of the Jews."

Then two bandits were crucified with him, one on his right and one on his left. Those who passed by derided him, shaking their heads and saying, "You who would destroy the temple and build it in three days, save yourself! If you are the Son of God, come down from the cross." In the same way the chief priests also, along with the scribes and elders, were mocking him, saying, "He saved others; he cannot save himself. He is the King of Israel; let him come down from the cross now, and we will believe in him. He trusts in God; let God deliver him now, if he wants to; for he said, 'I am God's Son.'" The bandits who were crucified with him also taunted him in the same way.

From noon on, darkness came over the whole land until three in the afternoon. And about three o'clock Jesus cried with a loud voice, "Eli, Eli, lema sabachthani?" that is, "My God, my God, why have you forsaken me?" When some of the bystanders heard it, they said, "This man is calling for Elijah." At once one of them ran and got a sponge, filled it with sour wine, put it on a stick, and gave it to him to drink. But the others said, "Wait, let us see whether Elijah will come to save him." Then Jesus cried again with a loud voice and breathed his last. At that moment the curtain of the temple was torn in two, from top to bottom. The earth shook, and the rocks were split. The tombs also were opened, and many bodies of the saints who had fallen asleep were raised. After his resurrection they came out of the tombs and entered the holy city and appeared to many. Now when the centurion and those with him, who were keeping watch over Jesus, saw the earthquake and what took place, they were terrified and said, "Truly this man was God's Son!"

Many women were also there, looking on from a distance; they had followed Jesus from Galilee and had provided for him. Among them were Mary Magdalene, and Mary the mother of James and Joseph, and the mother of the sons of Zebedee.

TO PONDER: Romans 8:11-17, Psalm 31:5, Matthew 10:38, Matthew 16:24, Mark 8:34, Luke 9:23, Luke 14:27, Mark 15:33-34, Luke 23:32-49, John 19:23-37

LECTIO DIVINA

THE CRUCIFIXION | MATTHEW 27:35-56

LECTIO

Matthew's overriding theme is that Jesus is truly the promised Messiah, the fulfillment of the Old Testament prophecies. The mocking crowd, the dividing of His clothes, and Christ's cry of abandonment, as well as other details, are direct fulfillments of Old Testament prophecies. Even the natural world bears witness to the death of God: the earth quakes and the sun disappears, leading to the centurion's confession of faith.

MEDITATIO

What personal message does the text have for me?

ORATIO

What do I say to the Lord in response to His word?

CONTEMPLATIO

What conversion of mind, heart, and life is He asking of me today?

How did I progress in living the Word today?

THE FIFTH SORROWFUL MYSTERY: THE CRUCIFIXION

I remember that day like none other during my cancer treatment. I was in tremendous pain when I got there—chemotherapy had so shredded the inside of my gut that I felt like I was in the final throes of unmedicated childbirth. This drug-induced side effect was the worst pain I've ever experienced, and my gut still bears the scars. When I remember though, it is not the pain that stands in stark relief. It is the sense of being at once intensely lonely and filled completely.

Rarely during my treatment did I travel to the hospital alone. My husband was with me for every chemotherapy treatment, and his father took me to every radiation treatment. On this day, though, I went by myself. I was there to be tattooed so that shields could be aligned and protect my organs from the damaging rays of radiation. My job was to lie still, arms akimbo, chest bared, on the cold metal table while someone inked tiny dots all over my torso. My body sports more tattoos than my well-tatted son's, all so small that they bear nearly-private witness to my nearly-private agony.

I walked into that room already in pain, the kind of pain that would best be described as "writhing pain." But I could not move. The accuracy of the shields was dependent on my stillness. There, naked and in pain, I couldn't help but think of our Lord as He was nailed to the cross. He was all I could think of. His pain was so much more than mine. I was in that room to save my own life. He allowed Himself to be nailed to the cross not to save Himself, but to offer me life beyond death. I pondered the crucifixion and felt the wounds of Christ.

When I returned home after the ordeal, my husband was there with our toddler son and his parents. He looked up briefly and asked how it went. I could barely speak for the horror.

"It was awful."

No one in the room had anything to say. All attention reverted to the toddler in order to fill the awkward void where words could neither convey nor console the suffering. No one would ever share that experience with me except Jesus. Even now, I cannot adequately express the intense pain or the intense intimacy with the Consoler.

We all have experiences of suffering—some physical, some emotional. Jesus did not come to live and die among us in order to save us from suffering. He came to save us from the fires of hell, not the pain of the cross. Actually, He tells us that we will have choose to die to ourselves in order to live forever in Him. To walk with Him in this life, we will carry crosses. God wants us to understand this so clearly that His words are recorded twice in Matthew and Luke and once in Mark.

We are assured, though, that as Christians, the same God who hung on the cross and died for us is with us when we suffer. He knows our pain and His suffering gives us life. Saint Teresa Benedicta (Edith Stein) writes: "The soul was created for union with God through the cross, redeemed by the cross, consumed and sanctified by the cross, so that it would be marked with the sign of the cross for all eternity."

Of my cancer experience, I've often said that I am grateful for the ways it shaped my soul, but that I hope never to embrace that particular cross again. With nearly thirty years of perspective, I see how God used that cross in my life, a cross perfectly designed to bring me into His presence in an exquisitely intimate way.

In the most intense pain, it is likely we will find ourselves completely alone, save for the crucified Jesus. He is the only one who can speak into that kind of death. He is the only one who truly knows the cost. And He is the only who can console.

My prayer as I ponder this mystery with you is that the God who hung for us will meet us in our most excruciating pain and leave His indelible mark of love on our souls.

Elizabeth Foss

ACTIO

How will I make my life a gift for others in charity?
What does God want me to do today?

GRACE

As you ponder the crucifix, don't turn away. What is He saying to you as you
look on Him in His agony?

GIFT

Notice what is lacking. Donate your time, your money, your food, your
service. Meet a real physical need today.

GRATITUDE

Thank you, Lord, for these blessings:

PRAY THE ROSARY

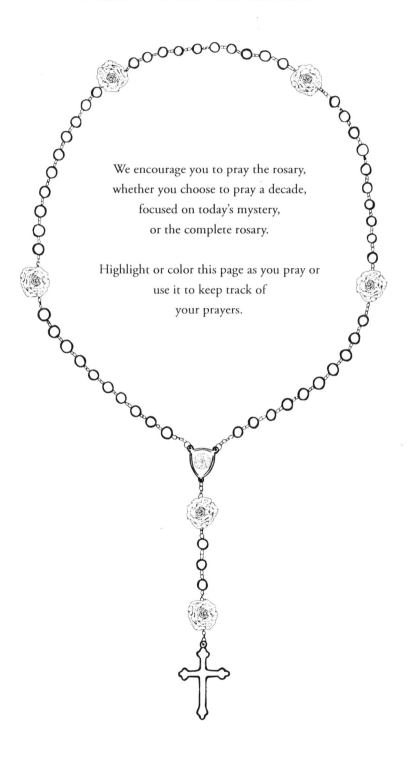

We encourage you to pray the rosary,
whether you choose to pray a decade,
focused on today's mystery,
or the complete rosary.

Highlight or color this page as you pray or
use it to keep track of
your prayers.

Selah

DAY TWENTY-ONE

Selah is a Hebrew word found often in the psalms and a few times in Habakkuk. Scholars aren't absolutely certain what it means. It seems to be a musical or liturgical note—maybe a pause or maybe a crescendo.

We have set aside this space—this day—for you to use as your selah. Perhaps you pause here and just review what you have pondered thus far. Perhaps you rejoice here and use the space for shouts of praise. Or maybe you take the opportunity to fill in some gaps in the pages before this one.

It's your space.

Selah.

Give it meaning.

The Sorrowful Mysteries

Botanical Bouquet

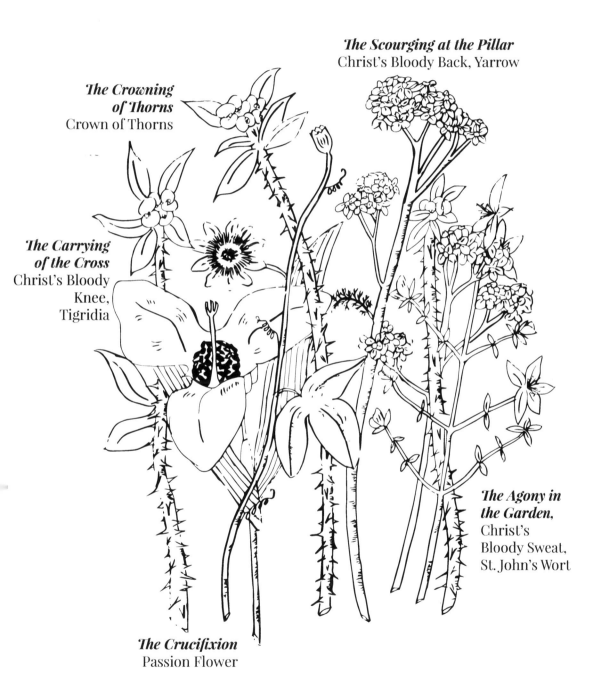

The Scourging at the Pillar
Christ's Bloody Back, Yarrow

**The Crowning
of Thorns**
Crown of Thorns

**The Carrying
of the Cross**
Christ's Bloody
Knee,
Tigridia

**The Agony in
the Garden,**
Christ's
Bloody Sweat,
St. John's Wort

The Crucifixion
Passion Flower

THE

GLORIOUS MYSTERIES

WEEKLY SCRIPTURE MEMORY

THE GLORIOUS MYSTERIES

With the glorious mysteries, we rejoice in the fullness of the Gospel. Our home is with our Creator and our Jesus has made it so that we will live with Him forever in heaven. *So, do not be troubled.*

John 14:1-3

"Do not let your hearts be troubled. Believe in God, believe also in me. In my Father's house there are many dwelling places. If it were not so, would I have told you that I go to prepare a place for you? And if I go and prepare a place for you, I will come again and will take you to myself, so that where I am, there you may be also."

do not let your hearts be troubled.

JOHN 14:1

DAY TWENTY-THREE

JOHN 20:1-18

Early on the first day of the week, while it was still dark, Mary Magdalene came to the tomb and saw that the stone had been removed from the tomb. So she ran and went to Simon Peter and the other disciple, the one whom Jesus loved, and said to them, "They have taken the Lord out of the tomb, and we do not know where they have laid him." Then Peter and the other disciple set out and went toward the tomb. The two were running together, but the other disciple outran Peter and reached the tomb first. He bent down to look in and saw the linen wrappings lying there, but he did not go in. Then Simon Peter came, following him, and went into the tomb. He saw the linen wrappings lying there, and the cloth that had been on Jesus' head, not lying with the linen wrappings but rolled up in a place by itself. Then the other disciple, who reached the tomb first, also went in, and he saw and believed; for as yet they did not understand the scripture, that he must rise from the dead. Then the disciples returned to their homes.

But Mary stood weeping outside the tomb. As she wept, she bent over to look into the tomb; and she saw two angels in white, sitting where the body of Jesus had been lying, one at the head and the other at the feet. They said to her, "Woman, why are you weeping?" She said to them, "They have taken away my Lord, and I do not know where they have laid him." When she had said this, she turned around and saw Jesus standing there, but she did not know that it was Jesus. Jesus said to her, "Woman, why are you weeping? Whom are you looking for?" Supposing him to be the gardener, she said to him, "Sir, if you have carried him away, tell me where you have laid him, and I will take him away." Jesus said to her, "Mary!" She turned and said to him in Hebrew, "Rabbouni!" (which means Teacher). Jesus said to her, "Do not hold on to me, because I have not yet ascended to the Father. But go to my brothers and say to them, 'I am ascending to my Father and your Father, to my God and your God.'" Mary Magdalene went and announced to the disciples, "I have seen the Lord"; and she told them that he had said these things to her.

TO PONDER: Matthew 28:1-10, Mark 16:1-8, Luke 24:1-12, 1 Corinthians 15:3-8, Mark 9:23-25

LECTIO DIVINA

THE RESURRECTION | JOHN 20:1-23

Mary Magdalene's deep love for Jesus drives her actions—to stay with Him as He preached, as He died on the cross, and now, as she searches for His missing body. Her weeping turns to joy when Jesus appears before her, alive! She is blessed with this first appearance of her resurrected God. Her profound joy is the fruit of her equally profound love and devotion.

What personal message does the text have for me?

What do I say to the Lord in response to His word?

What conversion of mind, heart, and life is He asking of me today?

How did I progress in living the Word today?

THE FIRST GLORIOUS MYSTERY:
THE RESURRECTION

Where are you, Lord?

This question resounds repeatedly in my heart like the reverberation of a steadily beating drum. I search frantically for the answers, a justification, any bit of meaning to make sense of the behavior of another that has left me emotionally wrecked. I cannot comprehend what has occurred, but it is all I desire in the moment.

I cannot find peace, but that is my own doing. My faith is weak. I grasp for a solution of my own accord, attempting to force a resolution.

Mary Magdalene is at the tomb when it is discovered that Jesus is no longer there. She yearns to make sense of it all. She posits the only sensible explanation—surely, someone has taken Him away elsewhere. A dead man could not simply get up and walk off.

Yet, there is room in her heart for another possibility. Her faith stretches her heart open wide enough for a solution her head won't quite be able to fathom (in this life).

She recognizes Him at the sound of His voice calling her name gently. It is not a physical recognition, but one in her innermost being.

The Lord calls out to each of us in this manner, too. It is in the quiet recesses of our heart, open to hearing His voice, that He whispers our names and speaks to us. But we are only able to hear it with a receptive heart. One who is so hardened in the stubbornness of "my way or the highway" can't discern His voice calling out. Similarly, one who is chattering so loudly interiorly (or exteriorly) that He doesn't have a chance to get a word in edgewise is not well-disposed to perceiving His voice through the cacophony.

Mary still doesn't understand what has happened, but she steps forward in faith. Her eagerness is apparent; Jesus has to halt her steps and soften her zeal. She is ready when the apostles are not. She is present; they have become anxious and have flitted away. Their preconceived notions about how things will unfold do not give them the eyes to see and the ears to hear the Lord presently. These things must be stripped away before they are prepared to see Him in His resurrected glory.

Faith waits for the right moment. It does not attempt to force the explanation, the event, the exchange on one's own time. Faith makes us prepared for that moment when it comes. A heart readied and steadied in faith will be open to the revelation when it happens, just as it is meant to happen.

Faith is that small seed tenderly placed in the soil, fertilized by the sacraments, watered by works of mercy, warmed by encounters with the Son. It is tiny, yet it persists. We see it at work when Mary Magdalene, not understanding where her Lord could be, remains unrelenting in her search and available until He reveals Himself to her in His own time, in His own way.

At the very core of a resurrection sort of faith is the ability to believe in the impossible. Men are not supposed to come back to life once they have died. They certainly aren't capable of entering into the realm of divine life which is above and beyond their nature. And yet, here He is. Fully man, risen from the dead, brought into the fullness of life.

The Lord, too, was present with me in my pain, in my incomprehensibility, but I had to quiet my one-sided conversation and open my heart to hear His voice leading me to a place of healing and peace. I stepped out in humble, trusting, determined faith. He moved mountains. (Matthew 17:20)

And He will move that mountain for you, too. Step out in faith.

Laurel Muff

ACTIO

How will I make my life a gift for others in charity?
What does God want me to do today?

GRACE

Wait. Identify one area of your life where you will wait in tender surrender.

GIFT

Resurrect a relationship today. Reach out to someone you haven't connected with in a while, but who will be grateful to know you remembered she or he has had meaning in your life.

GRATITUDE

Thank you, Lord, for these blessings:

PRAY THE ROSARY

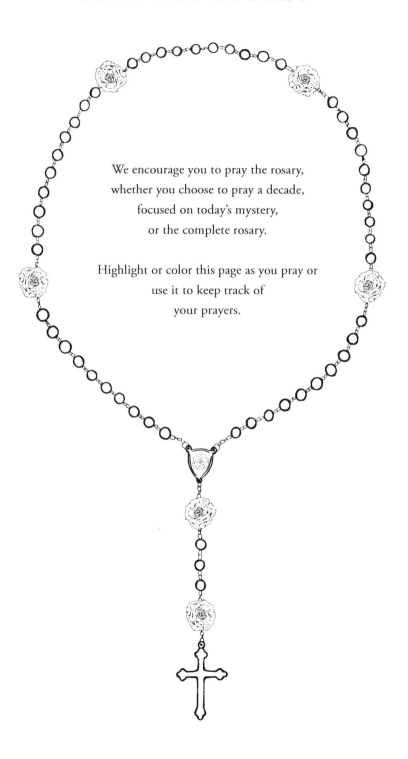

We encourage you to pray the rosary,
whether you choose to pray a decade,
focused on today's mystery,
or the complete rosary.

Highlight or color this page as you pray or
use it to keep track of
your prayers.

MATTHEW 28:16-20

Now the eleven disciples went to Galilee, to the
mountain to which Jesus had directed them. When
they saw him, they worshiped him; but some doubted.
And Jesus came and said to them, "All authority
in heaven and on earth has been given to me. Go
therefore and make disciples of all nations, baptizing
them in the name of the Father and of the Son and of
the Holy Spirit, and teaching them to obey everything
that I have commanded you. And remember, I am
with you always, to the end of the age."

TO PONDER: Mark 16:19-20, Luke 24:50-53, Acts 1:1-11

LECTIO DIVINA

THE ASCENSION | MATTHEW 28:16-20

These verses, from the end of Matthew's gospel, illustrate that God will always be with His people. While Jesus ascends to His heavenly glory, He does not leave the apostles, or the Church, alone—He will be with them (and us) always. And He has given us all a task: to make disciples of all nations, converting entire cultures to life under the Lordship of Christ and the gospel message.

MEDITATIO

What personal message does the text have for me?

ORATIO

What do I say to the Lord in response to His word?

CONTEMPLATIO

What conversion of mind, heart, and life is He asking of me today?

How did I progress in living the Word today?

THE SECOND GLORIOUS MYSTERY:
THE ASCENSION OF JESUS

"You need to come to the ICU right away," my brother said over the phone. "He's not going to make it much longer."

I stood in my girlfriend's kitchen with my two elementary-aged children, clutching their small hands. My father was dying with only hours left this side of heaven. He'd come to the end of his courageous ten year battle with non-Hodgkin's lymphoma and it was time to let him go home to his heavenly Father.

As I made my way to the hospital, begging God to keep Dad here long enough for me to say goodbye, my heart banged around in my chest. I gripped the wheel but still weaved in my lane. I had to do something to calm myself down. So, just like my dad had taught me, I found my rosary tucked into my cup holder and I began to pray, interceding for him with every Hail Mary and Glory Be.

My dad loved the Blessed Mother and prayed the rosary daily. When cancer invaded his body, he had trouble holding the small beads so my mother found him one with larger beads to make it easier. He kept it under his pillow so when he woke up in the middle of the night fighting nausea or pain, there was comfort among the beads.

I made it to the hospital in time to say everything before my father took his last breath. He was surrounded by five of his eight children and his wife of thirty-six years. While we prayed the rosary together, my mother announced that it was Ascension Thursday.

May 24, 2001—Ascension Thursday—was my father's heavenly homecoming. As my dad passed, that glorious mystery came to life. I imagined what Dad must be seeing—Jesus walking toward him, holding His arms wide open to welcome him home.

When I read this scripture passage from Matthew, I imagine the apostles felt the same way about watching Jesus ascend into heaven. There was doubt, pain, and joy in witnessing the great goodbye. And when my dad died, I also felt all those emotions. I wanted my father to stay, but I didn't have a choice. God's plan was unfolding and I was being asked to trust that all would be well.

Later that evening, as my brothers, sister, and I gathered at my parents' home, I shared my heart with my mother. Who were we without Dad here? He was a magnanimous, big-hearted man who took over a room and drew people to him. The acute pain over the thought of never hearing his laughter or his booming voice again almost broke me. My eyes spilled over and my mother pulled me into her arms and whispered, "Dad will remain in your heart, Mary Beth. He will always be with you. Like Jesus said before his Ascension, I am with you always, to the end of age."

I don't believe it was a coincidence that my father died on this feast day. His love for the Lord and his special devotion to our Lady were on full display as he made his journey home to God. His legacy was left within the hearts of his children, who have joyfully passed it on to another generation.

As you ponder this glorious mystery, remember the legacy of Jesus, now passed down for 2,000 years. How humbled and joy-filled the apostles were when they left that mountain. They had chosen to follow Jesus and, even though He was no longer physically with them, everything He had taught them was called forth, so they could go and preach the Good News. Just like my father passed his legacy of love and faith to his children, Jesus passes His legacy on to us.

Even in the moments of doubt, we are reminded God never leaves us without hope. Let us call upon the lessons and legacy of Christ as we go forth to minister to those God has placed in our path.

Mary Lenaburg

ACTIO

How will I make my life a gift for others in charity?
What does God want me to do today?

GRACE

What is the personal legacy Jesus has passed to you?
How has He given you the gift of hope?

GIFT

Think of someone who has taught you about your faith in such a way that
it remains with you. Make a phone call or send a quick text, and let them
know that they remain with you today because of this.

GRATITUDE

Thank you, Lord, for these blessings:

PRAY THE ROSARY

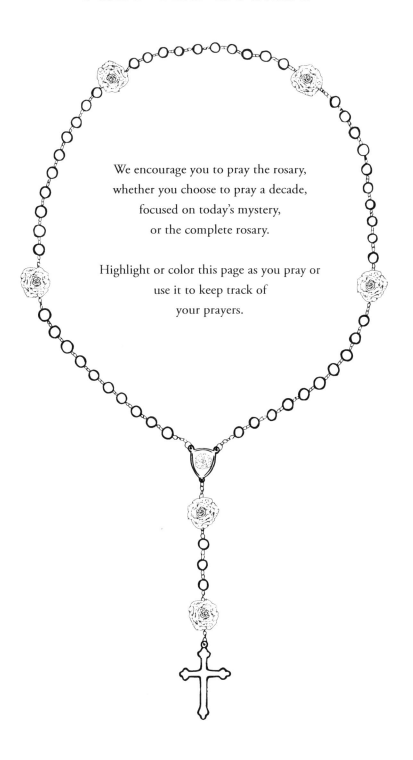

We encourage you to pray the rosary,
whether you choose to pray a decade,
focused on today's mystery,
or the complete rosary.

Highlight or color this page as you pray or
use it to keep track of
your prayers.

TAKE UP AND READ

DAY TWENTY-FIVE

ACTS 2:1-4

When the day of Pentecost had come, they were all together in one place. And suddenly from heaven there came a sound like the rush of a violent wind, and it filled the entire house where they were sitting. Divided tongues, as of fire, appeared among them, and a tongue rested on each of them. All of them were filled with the Holy Spirit and began to speak in other languages, as the Spirit gave them ability.

ACTS 2:43-47

They devoted themselves to the apostles' teaching and fellowship, to the breaking of bread and the prayers. Awe came upon everyone, because many wonders and signs were being done by the apostles. All who believed were together and had all things in common; they would sell their possessions and goods and distribute the proceeds to all, as any had need. Day by day, as they spent much time together in the temple, they broke bread at home and ate their food with glad and generous hearts, praising God and having the goodwill of all the people. And day by day the Lord added to their number those who were being saved.

TO PONDER: Isaiah 11:1-3, Acts 2:38-41, Romans 5:5, Ephesians 6:17, Luke 11:9-13, Romans 8:9

LECTIO DIVINA

THE DESCENT OF THE HOLY SPIRIT | ACTS 2:1-4, 43-47

Written around 63 A.D., the book of Acts was also written by Saint Luke. In writing Acts, Luke was mainly interested in the activity of the Holy Spirit, Who guided the Church's growth. In today's reading, Luke details the events of Pentecost, the day when the Holy Spirit descended upon the apostles and gave them the gifts they needed to begin spreading the gospel throughout the world.

What personal message does the text have for me?

What do I say to the Lord in response to His word?

What conversion of mind, heart, and life is He asking of me today?

How did I progress in living the Word today?

THE THIRD GLORIOUS MYSTERY:
THE DESCENT OF THE HOLY SPIRIT

I am a person who is most comfortable meeting God alone. I love my quiet time. I love my spiritual reading. I even love solitary walks where I recognize Him in His creation.

When I ponder Pentecost and the powerful effect it had on mankind, at first I am alarmed. This mystery pushes me out of my comfort zone. Where someone else may be more challenged by persecution or by the call to suffer alone, I struggle with the idea that the Holy Spirit most often makes Himself present in a group.

The disciples were all gathered together when the tongues of fire descended and the Holy Spirit rested upon them. He didn't meet each one individually. He met them corporately, in a group.

And the beautiful passage about wonders and signs? They were together—together in ministry, together in the temple, together in the celebration of the Eucharist, together in homes and around tables, together in prayer and in praise. Their joys were more joyful together; their griefs were more grace-filled together. The early Church did life together: they lived and served and prayed with one another intentionally and regularly. Luke doesn't just tell us that they worshiped together. He makes it abundantly clear the Spirit was made manifest in the midst of gatherings of two or more.

We are called to community. The Holy Spirit exists in community with the Father and the Son. The Trinity is for us the perfect community. When Jesus offered His holy sacrifice at the Last Supper, He commanded His disciples to continue the practice of breaking bread together in order to remember Him and to proclaim His death and resurrection until He returned. (1 Corinthians 11:23-26) He promised them the Holy Spirit and He also promised it would be better than when He was present with them in the flesh. He said, "It is to your advantage that I go away, for if I do not go away, the Counselor [the Holy Spirit] will not come to you; but if I go, I will send him to you." (John 16:7) Christ can be more intimately united to us through the Spirit than Jesus was with the disciples. He wants communion for us—Communion in the sacramental sense and communion with one another. It's a mandate, really. When two or more gathered, He is there. (Matthew 18:20) So gather frequently.

The early Church developed rhythms of being together in Jesus and with Jesus that we see in our liturgical practices today. But they didn't limit themselves to a once-a-week encounter with one another or with our Lord. They made a lifestyle out of coming together. With the gifts of the Holy Spirit, the Lord meets the needs of all of us through each other. He gives one person an abundance of one thing to fill what is lacking in someone else. This arrangement works well when we are in harmony with one another in the Church. When each believer acts in service to another, the Church thrives. The Church intentionally living together lives in the glory of God—everyone in awe of His goodness. God grew this joy through the ministry of each member to one another in genuine community.

Of course their numbers grew! Who wouldn't want to belong to a group such as this? The Holy Spirit was the force behind the growth of the Church then. He still is. His means to grow? Now, as then, the instruments of growth are those four critical elements: apostolic teaching, local fellowship, frequent celebration of the Eucharist, and fervent prayer. All four are most fertile when we gather.

I am devoted to prayer. And I am devoted to teaching. I hunger for the Eucharist and I know how to satiate that hunger. I wonder, though, what would the Holy Spirit do in my life if I were as devoted to local fellowship as I am to solitary pursuit of holiness? I wonder what He would do in yours?

Elizabeth Foss

ACTIO

How will I make my life a gift for others in charity?
What does God want me to do today?

GRACE

In what ways does the Holy Spirit call you out of your comfort zone?

GIFT

Write three short, encouraging notes to local people. Put them in envelopes.
Address them. Actually mail them. Alternatively, deliver them yourself.

GRATITUDE

Thank you, Lord, for these blessings:

PRAY THE ROSARY

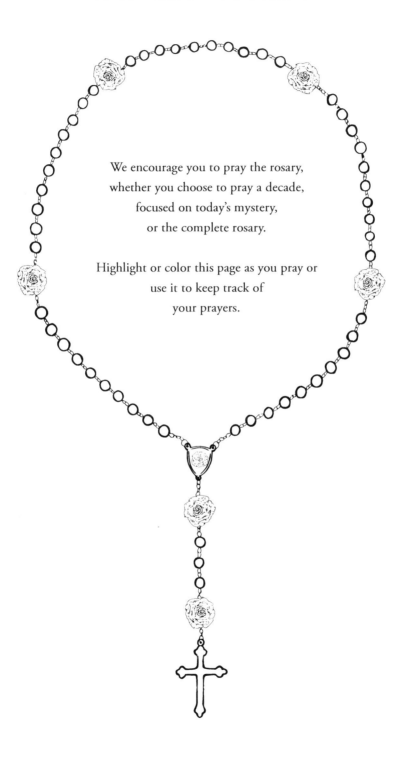

We encourage you to pray the rosary,
whether you choose to pray a decade,
focused on today's mystery,
or the complete rosary.

Highlight or color this page as you pray or
use it to keep track of
your prayers.

SONG OF SOLOMON 2:10-13

My beloved speaks and says to me:
"Arise, my love, my fair one,
   and come away;

for now the winter is past,
   the rain is over and gone.

The flowers appear on the earth;
   the time of singing has come,
and the voice of the turtledove
   is heard in our land.

The fig tree puts forth its figs,
   and the vines are in blossom;
   they give forth fragrance.
Arise, my love, my fair one,
   and come away."

TO PONDER: Psalm 45, Romans 5:8, Romans 8:28-32

LECTIO DIVINA

THE ASSUMPTION | SONG OF SOLOMON 2:10-13

Also called the "Song of Songs" and the "Canticle of Canticles", the author of this book is not definitively known, although it is traditionally credited to King Solomon, and is dated around the 10th century B.C. One of the wisdom books, it is a collection of romantic poetry that vividly illustrates the intimacy of human love, oriented toward marriage, and is a reflection of God's love for us.

What personal message does the text have for me?

What do I say to the Lord in response to His word?

What conversion of mind, heart, and life is He asking of me today?

How did I progress in living the Word today?

THE FOURTH GLORIOUS MYSTERY:
THE ASSUMPTION OF MARY

After His Ascension, Jesus must have been delighted. That's what heaven is about, isn't it? He was free from suffering, surrounded by angels, in the presence of the Father and the Spirit.

I think He missed His mom.

He was perfectly happy, I'm sure. But His infinite heart longed for the woman who had loved Him so well. As He watched her leading the Apostles, teaching them, telling them stories, He looked forward to the day she would come home.

So I can only imagine what heaven was like the day before the Assumption, the angels all abuzz with the news that the one before whom Gabriel bowed was coming soon. Soon the hands that held the Son would reach up to touch her starry crown. Soon the eyes that looked tearfully upon the cross would see all creation. Soon the womb that bore Him, the skin that stretched to contain the Creator of the stars, even the stretch marks themselves, would be glorified.

It's impossible to imagine this accurately, angels not having bodies and heaven not really being a place, but I think there was the angelic equivalent of bustling about cleaning and baking and decorating and fixing hair. I expect it had all the feeling of a palace preparing for a royal wedding.

And imagine His joy, as He called out, "Arise, my love, my fair one, and come away!" The love in His eyes as He looked on His mother. Think of the embrace, as He held her close after who knows how many years. I picture Him catching her up in His strong arms and spinning her around.

I think He longs for you just as much.

Overjoyed as He is to be in the presence of the Father, the Spirit, the angels, the saints, and the Queen of Heaven and Earth, there is room in His infinite heart to thirst for you.

And when you hear Him call you to arise and begin making your way home, heaven will be abuzz with the news of it, the angels and saints giddy to meet you, the Blessed Mother preparing a place for you. You will be clothed with robes all fragrant with myrrh and led with joy and gladness into the palace of the King.

Imagine His joy. Picture how He'll look at you, how He'll run to you, how He'll hold you.

The day you go home will be a royal wedding. There at the gates of heaven, your Beloved will meet you, embrace you, and make you His bride forever. "Arise, my love, my fair one, and come away." That's what it is to be a Christian: to be a child of the Father called to be the Bride of Christ.

This is what we're living for. This is the reason that we keep fighting for holiness: so that He can make us worthy to follow where Mary went. In meditating on the Assumption, we're thinking not only of Jesus' love for His mom but of His love for us. He aches to be with you, my friends. He's desperate to have you with Him forever.

Even better: this bridal love isn't just a promise for the future. Every time you receive Him in the Eucharist, you have a foretaste of that wedding feast. As you walk up the aisle to receive the Bridegroom who laid down His life for you, you are a bride preparing to be embraced with as much joy as Jesus had on the day of the Assumption. He delights in you on a random Tuesday in Ordinary Time just as much as He delighted in Mary when He brought her to heaven.

Today, take some time just to sit in this certainty: the God of the Universe loves you more passionately than any other man has ever loved his bride. Whatever life may be handing you today, you are unceasingly and inestimably loved.

Meg Hunter-Kilmer

ACTIO

How will I make my life a gift for others in charity?
What does God want me to do today?

GRACE

You are loved beyond measure by the God of the Universe. Do you feel
that excitement every time you walk down the aisle to receive Him in the
Eucharist?

GIFT

Today, take note of the unique gift of your feminine body. Do something
special to care for it: a good run, a manicure, a haircut, even an intentional
big bottle of water.

GRATITUDE

Thank you, Lord, for these blessings:

PRAY THE ROSARY

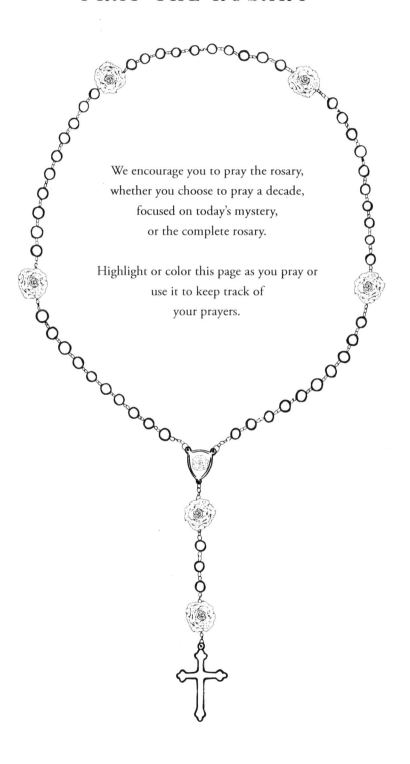

We encourage you to pray the rosary,
whether you choose to pray a decade,
focused on today's mystery,
or the complete rosary.

Highlight or color this page as you pray or
use it to keep track of
your prayers.

REVELATION 12:1-16

A great portent appeared in heaven: a woman clothed with the sun, with the moon under her feet, and on her head a crown of twelve stars. She was pregnant and was crying out in birth pangs, in the agony of giving birth. Then another portent appeared in heaven: a great red dragon, with seven heads and ten horns, and seven diadems on his heads. His tail swept down a third of the stars of heaven and threw them to the earth. Then the dragon stood before the woman who was about to bear a child, so that he might devour her child as soon as it was born. And she gave birth to a son, a male child, who is to rule all the nations with a rod of iron. But her child was snatched away and taken to God and to his throne; and the woman fled into the wilderness, where she has a place prepared by God, so that there she can be nourished for one thousand two hundred sixty days.

TO PONDER: Sirach 6:33-35, Sirach 3:17, Galatians 4:6-9

LECTIO DIVINA

THE CROWNING OF MARY QUEEN OF HEAVEN | REVELATION 12:1-6

Written by Saint John while exiled on the Greek island of Patmos in the late 90s A.D., the book of Revelation is the last book of the Bible. Its title comes from the Greek *apokálypsis*, meaning "revealing" or "unveiling", and it is the only example of apocalyptic literature in the New Testament. In Chapter 12, the "woman clothed with the sun" represents Mary, who gave birth to Jesus, the child who will rule all nations.

MEDITATIO

What personal message does the text have for me?

ORATIO

What do I say to the Lord in response to His word?

CONTEMPLATIO

What conversion of mind, heart, and life is He asking of me today?

How did I progress in living the Word today?

DAY TWENTY-SEVEN

155

THE FIFTH GLORIOUS MYSTERY:
THE CROWNING OF MARY QUEEN OF HEAVEN

I once had a somewhat startling discussion with my nana before she peacefully passed away in her nineties. Nana was a lifelong, devout Catholic, and my family's own little slice of faith personified. She was also a bit of a rebel. She earned her college degree back when very few women did and jokes she was an old maid by the time she got married at the ripe old age of twenty-six. She also defied family tradition, marrying a Protestant.

My dad always talks about my nana's unwavering faith, how she was very much like a handmaid of the Lord and so full of trust and acceptance even in the wake of suffering, so you can imagine how surprising it was when Nana confessed she had a hard time relating to the Mother of God.

She told me, "How could I relate to a mom of one – and the mom of God, a perfect son, no less?"

Nana, as amazingly faithful as she was, raised nine imperfect kids and, like the rest of poor humanity, she was not conceived without original sin.

When you consider Mary's many virtues (to name a few: most patient, most pure, and most faithful) as well as the fact that she was crowned Queen of Heaven and Earth, you can see where my nana was coming from.

Truth is, we rarely—if ever—live up to Mary's impressive résumé, but that's okay. Maybe that's the point actually. Yes, my nana was an imperfect woman raising imperfect children with an imperfect husband in an oftentimes messy house. But it was never Nana or her life's messiness that made her like our Blessed Mother; it was her acceptance of it all and her faith in her Father.

When I imagine Mary as a queen, a woman "clothed with the sun," it's easy to start to feel a little intimidated. But she doesn't want us to approach her as fearful subjects. She desires for us to come to her as her little children, unintimidated by her crown. Mary wants to be the Cause of Our Joy, not the Cause of Our Oh-My-Gosh-I-Am-So-Awful-I'm-Not-Anything-Like-Mary. Then she wants to take our unmanicured hand—and if you're like me, your nail-bitten-hand-because-I-can-be-an-anxious-stressball—and bring us to Jesus. She wants to reveal to us the love she knew in her womb, in her arms, and in her life.

This Mystical Rose, this Seat of Wisdom, is looking down on all of us—only she's not looking down like a conceited, self-serving monarch might with haughtiness. No, Mary's gazing at us as God did through the prophet Isaiah: "You are precious in my sight, and honored, and I love you." (Isaiah 43:4) She is looking at us as our mother and with the most loving and most hope-filled eyes in the world.

I also suspect sweet Mama Mary probably sometimes shakes her head sadly when she sees how so many of us are so caught up in the "image is everything" culture, desperately trying to control others' perceptions of us and to seek the ephemeral coronations of the world. Beauty Queen. Success Queen. Queen Pinterest Mommy. Queen #Fitspo. None of these has eternal value.

Can you imagine if our Blessed Mother had been more concerned with her reputation and how she appeared to others? Her yes—the fiat that brought us Jesus—would likely never have happened.

Mary was crowned Queen of Heaven and All the Saints, not because she looked the part or even played the part but because she accepted the role God had given her with grace and trust.

We are called to do no less—to accept our lowliness here in this broken world and to trust God's sometimes confusing and painful plan for us so that we may one day gather right alongside our Blessed Mother in the palace of heaven

Kate Wicker

ACTIO

How will I make my life a gift for others in charity?
What does God want me to do today?

GRACE

Do you let yourself imagine heaven? Put yourself in there now, gazing on
Mary, Queen of Heaven. What do you want to share with her?

GIFT

Buy a grocery store bouquet today. Give it away, one flower at a time.

GRATITUDE

Thank you, Lord, for these blessings:

PRAY THE ROSARY

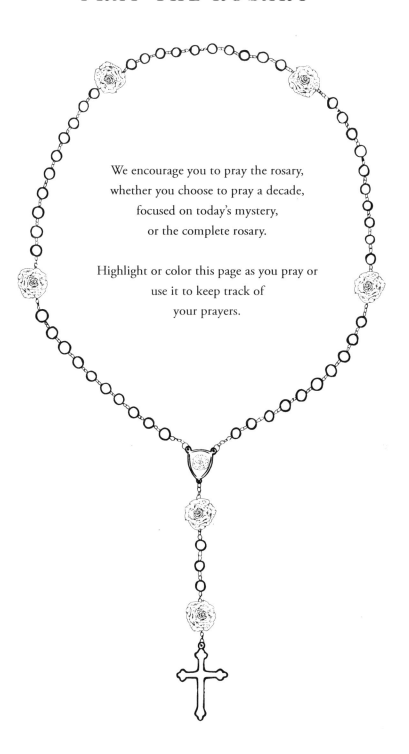

We encourage you to pray the rosary,
whether you choose to pray a decade,
focused on today's mystery,
or the complete rosary.

Highlight or color this page as you pray or
use it to keep track of
your prayers.

Selah

Selah is a Hebrew word found often in the psalms and a few times in Habakkuk. Scholars aren't absolutely certain what it means. It seems to be a musical or liturgical note—maybe a pause or maybe a crescendo.

We have set aside this space—this day—for you to use as your selah. Perhaps you pause here and just review what you have pondered thus far. Perhaps you rejoice here and use the space for shouts of praise. Or maybe you take the opportunity to fill in some gaps in the pages before this one.

It's your space.

Selah.

Give it meaning.

The Glorious Mysteries

Botanical Bouquet

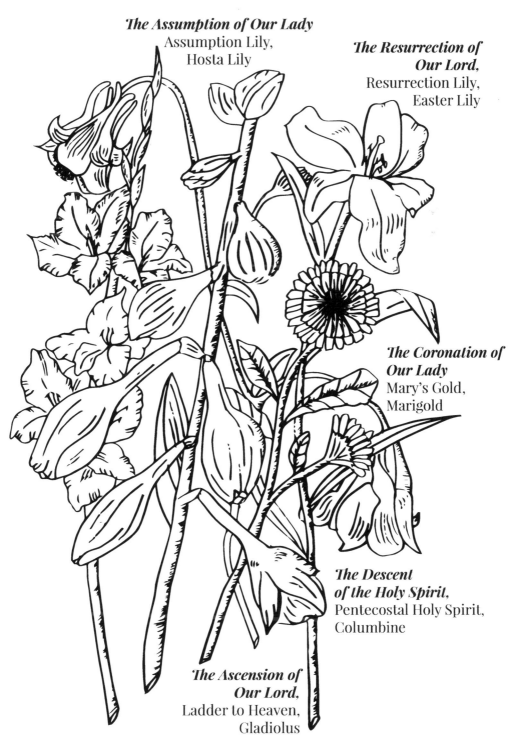

The Assumption of Our Lady
Assumption Lily,
Hosta Lily

**The Resurrection of
Our Lord,**
Resurrection Lily,
Easter Lily

**The Coronation of
Our Lady**
Mary's Gold,
Marigold

**The Descent
of the Holy Spirit,**
Pentecostal Holy Spirit,
Columbine

**The Ascension of
Our Lord,**
Ladder to Heaven,
Gladiolus

WHY LECTIO DIVINA?

Together, as a community of faithful women, we endeavor to better understand the heart of the gospel and to live it out in our lives. Each day, we invite our souls to encounter our Lord.

How? How will the tired soul living in the woman in the midst of secular culture and busyness still herself and find her Lord? How will she find hope and new energy in the act of one more thing on her to-do list?

She will pray—more. That's right. She will take more time to pray even though so many things pull on her time. Can we do that together? Can we take up for ourselves the ancient tradition of lectio divina and let the Word lead us to live in charity? We can and we must. This is the best way to prepare ourselves for each day with peaceful composure and serene grace.

In his 2010 apostolic exhortation *Verbum Domini*, Pope Benedict XVI beautifully instructs the faithful to prayerfully read the Scripture. Following his lead, we will be drawn into a practice that is as old as Scripture itself. We will closely read and ponder Scripture passages carefully chosen for this season.

In the early Christian communities, Scripture was read to nourish faith with the wisdom of truth. When we hold the New Testament, we take up the understanding that the first Christians had of the Old Testament, together with the divine revelation the Holy Spirit granted to Jesus' earliest followers.

The Church Fathers' faith was informed by their careful, prayerful reading of the Word. Today, we are blessed to welcome their wisdom into our reading when we access the commentaries that were the fruit of their lectio. The monastic movement grew in the fertile soil of lectio divina. The daily, ordered life of the monks was (and is) centered upon spiritual reading of Scripture. Can ordinary women in the twenty-first century find spiritual nourishment and new life in this age-old practice of holy men?

We can.

There are five steps in the pattern, five distinct movements that will direct the way we travel through our days. First, we read. Then, a meditation engages the mind, using reason to search for knowledge in the message. The prayer is the movement of the heart towards God, a beseeching on behalf of the soul. The contemplation elevates the mind and suspends it in God's presence. Finally, the action is the way we live our lives as a gift of charity towards others. It's a tall order, but it's the very best way to live.

Let's take a careful look at each step.

Pope Benedict writes, "It opens with the reading (lectio) of a text, which leads to a desire to understand its true content: what does the biblical text say in itself." (*Verbum Domini*, 87). This is where we explore the literary genre of the text, the characters we meet in the story, and the objective meaning intended by the author. We usually offer several passages which work together towards a common theme; you can choose just one passage, or you can look at the group together, as the Holy Spirit inspires. A good study Bible and/or a Bible dictionary will help you to place the reading in context.

"Next comes meditation (meditatio), which asks: what does the biblical text say to us?" (DV, 87) Prayerfully we ponder what personal message the text holds for each of us and what effect that message should have on our lives.

"Following this comes prayer (oratio), which asks the question: what do we say to the Lord in response to his word? Prayer, as petition, intercession, thanksgiving and praise, is the primary way by which the word transforms us." (DV, 87) What do we say to God in response to His Word? We ask Him what He desires of us. We ask Him for the strength and grace to do His will. Moved by His mercy, we give him thanks and praise.

The fourth act is "contemplation (contemplatio), during which we take up, as a gift from God, His own way of seeing and judging reality, and ask ourselves what conversion of mind, heart and life is the Lord asking of us?" (DV, 87) Here, reflect on how God has conveyed His love for us in the day's Scripture. Recognize the beauty of His gifts and the goodness of His mercy and rest in that. Let God light you from within and look out on the world in a new way because you have been transformed by the process of prayerful Scripture study.

Finally, the whole point of this time we've taken from our day is to get up from the reading and go live the Gospel. Actio is where we make an act of our wills and resolve to bring the text to life in our lives.

This is our fiat.

The process of lectio divina is not concluded until it arrives at action (actio), which moves the believer to make his or her life a gift for others in charity. We find the supreme synthesis and fulfillment of this process in the Mother of God. For every member of the faithful Mary is the model of docile acceptance of God's word, for she "kept all these things, pondering them in her heart."(Lk 2:19; cf. 2:51) (DV, 87)

As a community at Take Up & Read, we will endeavor to engage in lectio divina every day. To correlate with each day's Scripture passages, we've created pages for your time of prayer, and we've created pages for your active time. We want this book to come alive in your hands, to bring you a spiritual springtime. Try to take the time each day to dig deep, but if you have to cut your time short, don't be discouraged. Ask the Blessed Mother to help you find pockets throughout the day to re-engage. You don't have to fill in every box. There is no right or wrong answer. And you don't have to dig deeply with every passage.

Pray the parts you can, and trust the Holy Spirit to water it well in your soul. Know that God can do loaves and fishes miracles with your small parcels of time, if only you are willing to offer Him what you have. Before your days—and then your weeks—get swallowed with the ordinary to-do lists of life's hustle, sit in prayer and see how you can tune your heart to the beat of the Lord's, and ensure that the best gift you give is your life, poured out for others in charity.

NOTES

CARLY BUCKHOLZ studied poetry at the University of Virginia before earning a Master's in Higher Education. After five years in Charlottesville, she has moved across the Atlantic for a teaching fellowship in southern England. There, she teaches literature and works in student affairs. Often next to a pile of books, Carly spends most of her time trying to convince her friends to read more poetry and baking scones. She enjoys writing about her family, her faith, and the Blue Ridge Mountains.

MICAELA DARR lives in Southern California and is a happy wife to her husband, and mother to seven charming kiddos, ages twelve down to newborn. In her former life, she was an elementary and middle school teacher outside the home. Now, as a homeschooling mom, she does both those jobs (and many more) for far less money, but also more joy. She renewed her love of writing by starting a blog when her family took a two-year adventure to South Korea, and has since contributed her writing to several other Catholic websites, and two books set to be published in 2018-2019. Her latest out-of-the-home adventure is planning a small Catholic women's conference that aims to strengthen women on their journey to be closer to the God who loves them.

EMILY DeARDO is a lifelong Ohioan and the oldest of three children. Books—writing them, reading them, editing them, and talking about them—are her love language. Her first book, *Catholic 101*, was released in November 2017. When she's not reading, writing, or editing, Emily can be found re-reading Jane Austen, knitting, cheering for the Pittsburgh Penguins, drinking tea, or enjoying a meal with friends. To follow her adventures, visit her on Instagram at @emily_deardo, or at emilymdeardo.com.

ELIZABETH FOSS spends her days (and some nights) seeking beauty and truth and then searching for just the right words to express what she's found. The Founder and Content Director of Take Up & Read, she's astonished and incredibly grateful to have the opportunity to do work she loves with people she loves. Elizabeth lives in Loudoun County, Virginia with her husband and six of her nine kids, but frequently travels south to Charlottesville and north to New York and Connecticut to work (and play) with her grown children.

KATY GREINER is a freshly minted high school English teacher who's seeking peace amidst the healthy chaos change brings. When she's not looking over her shoulder for the real adult in the room to take care of her freshmen, she's planning trips or craving Chick-Fil-A. She loves a good sunset, great conversations, a strong cup of tea, all kinds of music, and hearing God laugh.

ANA HAHN is a wife of nine years and mother of five. She enjoys educating her three school-aged daughters at home and playing planes with her two toddler boys. In her rare spare time she works on making her home bright and cheerful and sharing bits of that, as well as other motherhood musings, on her blog, Time Flies When You're Having Babies.

ROSIE HILL lives on a farm in Virginia's Shenandoah Valley with her husband, mother, six small children, and a variety of animals. A former middle school music teacher, she now channels that energy into homeschooling and attempting to emulate Maria von Trapp (minus the curtain dresses). Her great loves in life include baking (and eating) fresh bread, reading beautiful books, singing sacred music, playing the ukulele (poorly), parenthetical remarks, and the Oxford comma.

MEG HUNTER-KILMER is a Virginia native who spent her college and graduate years at the University of Notre Dame, earning two degrees in theology. She spent time as a high school teacher before following God's call and becoming a hobo missionary, living out of her car. After years of stuffing her possessions into suitcases and travelling around the world teaching others about Jesus, she's currently settled down in Texas, writing for various online publications, working on her first book, and contributing to Take Up & Read studies. She blogs at www.piercedhands.com

MARY LENABURG is a writer, speaker, wife, and mother who travels around the country sharing her testimony about God's redeeming love and being brave in the scared. Mary currently works at Tepeyac OB-GYN, a pro-life medical practice near her home in Northern Virginia. She lives with her husband of twenty-nine years and her grown son and continues to embrace her father's advice: "Never quit, never give up, never lose your faith. It's the one reason you walk this earth. For God chose this time and place just for you, so make the most of it."

ALLISON MCGINLEY lives with her husband and two children in Northern Virginia. When she's not dancing with her daughter or learning about Legos from her son, she writes, sings with a local worship band, and takes pictures of beautiful things. She shares her photography and reflections on Instagram @allisonbenotafraid, and you can find her inspirational photography prints in her Etsy shop at benotafraidprints.com.

COLLEEN MITCHELL is a bringer-upper of boys, Gospel adventurer, wanna-be saint, author, and speaker. She is the author, of the award-winning *Who Does He Say You Are: Women Transformed by Christ in the Gospels*, and *When We Were Eve: Uncovering the Woman God Created You to Be*. Her latest adventure has taken her from the jungle of Costa Rica to the wilds of a sixth grade classroom in Fort Wayne, Indiana, where she is still living her mission to give everyone she meets just a little Jesus.

LAUREL MUFF is a California girl who loves to travel, write, knit, read, and sing (but not necessarily in that order). She is married to her best friend and they have two beautiful girls together, whom she teaches at home. She loves to gather people around the table for delicious food and great conversation. With a heart for ministry, she is glad to share her faith in whatever capacity the Lord beckons her. She shares her musings on her blog: muffindome.com.

HEATHER RENSHAW is a wife and mother of five living in the missionary territory of the Pacific Northwest. She loves deep conversation, loud singing, good eating, and silent Adoration. Heather is the author of an eight-week study on the Beatitudes, contributing author of *All Things Girl: Truth for Teens*, and is currently writing her first solo book for Catholic mothers called *Death By Minivan*. When she's not tackling the myriad tasks of her domestic church, Heather enjoys speaking at events, connecting via Twitter + Instagram (@RealCatholicMom), and dreaming big dreams. Heather may be found at www.RealCatholicMom.com

GINNY SHELLER lives with her husband and eight children in Virginia. They keep bees, goats, and chickens and rarely have a clean house or a quiet moment. Ginny knits every day to maintain sanity, and shares her family's life in words and pictures on her blog, Small Things, at www.gsheller.com.

KATE WICKER is a Catholic wife, mom of five, recovering perfectionist, speaker, and the author of *Getting Past Perfect: How to Find Joy & Grace in the Messiness of Motherhood* and *Weightless: Making Peace with Your Body*. When she's not playing the role of Uber driver, cook, or dispute resolution expert, Kate regularly contributes to myriad Catholic media. Her passion is encouraging women from all walks of life to reclaim the beauty of Creation and to recognize their worth. To learn more about her work and life, check out her highlight reel on Instagram (@KateWicker), or visit KateWicker.com.

KRISTIN FOSS is the Art Director and Designer. She is a self-taught watercolor artist who focuses on bright hues and details. With a paintbrush in her hand and fresh blooms in a vase, she finds peace in God's word while putting brush to paper. She lives in New England with her four children and husband, and loves escaping to the beach and exploring the city. She enjoys creative cooking, thrift stores, nature walks, water, and cotton.

KATRINA HARRINGTON is a wife, mother of four, and artist who can be found constantly pinching herself over getting to paint for a living. Her desk might appear to be rather haphazard, but, don't worry, she knows where everything is! Katrina first declared she wanted to be an artist in preschool, but she didn't realize the dream until she was twenty-five with two toddler boys at her knees and a little one on the way. Her first attempts at watercolor were with a garage sale paint kit courtesy of her bargain-hunting mother. Through her art shop, Rose Harrington, she seeks to blend the subtle and the profound through botanical theological symbolism and the wisdom of the saints. Katrina grew up showing chickens at the state fair, and her favorite dessert is fried bananas. She shares about her family's life on her blog, Cedars and Tiny Flowers.

RAKHI McCORMICK is a Catholic convert from Hinduism and a self-taught, aspiring artist specializing in lettering and whimsical illustrations. Her desire is to spread light into dark places with her art and photography, which can be found in her Etsy shop, Rakstar Designs. Rakhi is happiest alongside her family with a coffee in one hand and a pencil in the other (though fresh floral bouquets are lovely too!). She lives in the Metro Detroit area with her husband and three children and on Instagram at @rakstardesigns.

BIBLIOGRAPHY

The Bible. She Reads Truth Christian Standard Bible. Holman Bible Publishers, 2017.

The Didache Bible: With Commentaries Based on the Catechism of the Catholic Church. Ignatius Press, 2015.

The Navarre Bible: New Testament. Scepter Publishers, 2008.

Benedict XVI. *Jesus of Nazareth: Holy Week: From the Entrance into Jerusalem to the Resurrection*. Ignatius Press, 2011.

Catechism of the Catholic Church. http://www.vatican.va/archive/index.htm. Accessed March 1, 2018. http://www.vatican.va/archive/ENG0015/_INDEX.HTM

Escriva, Josemaria. *The Holy Rosary*. www.escrivaworks.org. Accessed February 19, 2018. http://www.escrivaworks.org/book/-point-3.htm

Groeschel, Fr. Benedict, C.F.R. *The Rosary: Chain of Hope*. Ignatius Press, 2003.

Hahn, Scott, general editor. *Catholic Bible Dictionary*. Doubleday Religion, 2009.

Hahn, Scott, editor, and Curtis Mitch, compiler. *Ignatius Catholic Study Bible: New Testament*. Ignatius Press, 2010.

John Paul II. *Letter to Women*. w2.vatican.va. June 29, 1995. Accessed February 19, 2018. https://w2.vatican.va/content/john-paul-ii/en/letters/1995/documents/hf_jp-ii_let_29061995_women.html

Kreeft, Peter. *Catholic Christianity*. Ignatius Press, 2001.

Lewis, Clive Staples. *Voyage of the Dawn Treader*. Harper Trophy, 2005.

Pius XI. *Quas Primas*. (On the Feast of Christ the King) w2.vatican.va. December 11 1925. Accessed February 19, 2018. http://w2.vatican.va/content/pius-xi/en/encyclicals/documents/hf_p-xi_enc_11121925_quas-primas.html

Stein, Edith. *The Science of the Cross: Collected Works of Edith Stein, Volume 6*. ICS Publications, 2011.

COLOPHON

This book was printed by CreateSpace, on 55# paper with an interior black and white.
Typefaces used include Adobe Garamond Pro and Serenity.
The cover is printed in full color with a soft touch matte, full laminate.
Finished size is 7" x 10".

Made in the USA
Middletown, DE
07 May 2018